JOURNAL OF AMERICAN INDIAN EDUCATION
Volume 56, Number 2
Summer 2017

The *Journal of American Indian Education* (ISSN 0021-8731) is published three times a year in spring, summer, and fall by the University of Minnesota Press, 111 Third Avenue South, Suite 290, Minneapolis, MN 55401-2520. http://www.upress.umn.edu

Copyright 2017 by the Arizona Board of Regents.

All rights reserved. With the exception of fair use, no part of this publication may be reproduced, stored in a retrieval system, or transmitted, in any form or by any means, electronic, mechanical, photocopying, recording, or otherwise, without a license or authorization from the Copyright Clearance Center (CCC) or the prior written permission of the University of Minnesota Press.

Postmaster: Send address changes to *JAIE*, University of Minnesota Press, 111 Third Avenue South, Suite 290, Minneapolis, MN 55401-2520.

Inquiries about manuscript submissions should be sent to jaie@asu.edu. Further information about manuscript submission is in the back of this issue and available online at https://jaie.asu.edu/content/submit-manuscript.

Address subscription orders, changes of address, and business correspondence (including requests for permission and advertising orders) to *JAIE*, University of Minnesota Press, 111 Third Avenue South, Suite 290, Minneapolis, MN 55401-2520.

Subscriptions: Regular U.S. rates: individuals, 1 year (3 issues) $35; libraries, 1 year $75. Other countries add $5 for each year's subscription. Checks should be made payable to the University of Minnesota Press. Back issues published after 2014: $20 (plus $6 shipping for the first copy, $1.25 for each additional copy inside the United States; $9.50 shipping for the first copy, $6 for each additional copy outside the United States). Back issues published before 2015: Please contact jaie@asu.edu.

Digital subscriptions to the *Journal of American Indian Education* are available online through the JSTOR Current Scholarship Program at http://www.jstor.org/r/umnpress.

Editors

Bryan McKinley Jones Brayboy
(Lumbee)
Arizona State University

K. Tsianina Lomawaima
(Mvskoke/Creek Nation)
Arizona State University

Teresa L. McCarty
University of California, Los Angeles

Jeston Morris (Diné)
Assistant Editor

Andrea Underwood
Business Manager

JAIE Editors Emeriti

David Beaulieu
(White Earth Chippewa)

Karen Gayton Comeau
(Standing Rock Sioux)

John W. Tippeconnic III (Comanche)

Octaviana Trujillo (Yoeme)

Denis Viri

Editorial Board

Seth A. Agbo
Lakehead University

Jo-ann Archibald (Stol:lo)
University of British Columbia

Megan Bang (Anishinabe)
University of Washington

Ray Barnhardt
University of Alaska, Fairbanks

Angelina E. Castagno
Northern Arizona University

Serafín M. Coronel-Molina
(Wanka/Quechua)
Indiana University

George Sefa Dei
University of Toronto

Susan C. Faircloth (Coharie)
University of North Carolina, Wilmington

Perry Gilmore
University of Arizona

Sandy Grande (Quechua)
Connecticut College

Justin Guillory (Nez Perce)
Northwest Indian College

Mary Hermes (Dakota, Chinese)
University of Minnesota

Beverly Klug
Idaho State University

Tiffany S. Lee (Diné-Lakota)
University of New Mexico

Beth Leonard (Deg Xinag Athabaskan)
University of Alaska, Fairbanks

Allan Luke
Queensland University of Technology

Margaret J. Maaka (Māori)
University of Hawai'i at Mānoa

Ananda M. Marin (Choctaw descent)
University of California, Los Angeles

Stephen May
University of Auckland

Douglas L. Medin
Northwestern University

Sharon Nelson-Barber (Rappahannock)
WestEd

Sheilah Nicholas (Hopi)
University of Arizona

Jon Reyhner
Northern Arizona University

Monty Roessel (Diné)
Diné College

Mary Eunice Romero-Little (Cochiti)
Arizona State University

Heather Shotton (Wichita/Kiowa/Cheyenne)
University of Oklahoma

Graham Smith (Māori)
Te Whare Wananga o Awanuiarangi

Linda Tuhiwai Smith (Māori)
University of Waikato

Elizabeth Sumida Huaman
(Wanka/Quechua)
Arizona State University

Eve Tuck (Aleut)
University of Toronto

Malia Villegas (Alutiiq/Sugpiaq)
Afognak Native Corporation

Stephanie Waterman (Onondaga)
University of Toronto

K. Laiana Wong (Native Hawaiian)
University of Hawai'i at Mānoa

Leisy T. Wyman
University of Arizona

Tarajean Yazzie-Mintz (Diné)
American Indian College Fund

VOLUME 56, ISSUE 2 2017

Editors' Introduction   1
BRYAN McKINLEY JONES BRAYBOY, K. TSIANINA LOMAWAIMA, AND TERESA L. McCARTY

Features

Use of Native Language and Culture (NLC) in Elementary and Middle School Instruction as a Predictor of Mathematics Achievement   3
MARK J. VAN RYZIN AND CLAUDIA G. VINCENT

Authentically Authored Native American Young Adult Literature (YAL) and Culturally Sustaining Pedagogy (CSP) in the Preparation of Preservice Teachers   34
ALICE HAYS

Learning Through Language: Academic Success in an Indigenous Language Immersion Kindergarten   57
LINDSAY A. MORCOM AND STEPHANIE ROY

Editors' Introduction

WELCOME TO THE SUMMER ISSUE of 2017. Three feature articles focus our attention on processes within the classroom and their impacts on various students in a variety of settings. We hope you enjoy these articles that share a thoughtful approach to evaluating pedagogical efficacy from kindergarten through elementary and middle school and into university level classrooms. The authors consistently set a high bar for considering the details of context in our research and for remembering the diversity of experiences and attitudes that all students bring to all classrooms.

The article by Mark J. Van Ryzin and Claudia G. Vincent follows up research published in 2016, in *JAIE* Volume 55, Issue 1, "Initial exploration of a construct representing Native language and culture (NLC) in elementary and middle school instruction," by Van Ryzin, Vincent, and Hoover. In the present issue, where they report on phase 2 of their research, Van Ryzin and Vincent tackle the findings of other scholars in large-scale studies that describe how integrating NLC into instruction in elementary and middle school math classes can negatively impact the achievement of Native students. They found that NLC impacts vary according to how strongly students' families identify with their Native culture and to the percentage of Native enrollment in schools. Their study demonstrates that using NLC may be more effective for students whose family and school contexts reflect more Native-centric cultural identification. Van Ryzin and Vincent raise important issues about attending to diversity in schools and homes and in designing research that takes into account the nuanced differences of context that influence student achievement.

Alice Hays turns our attention to college students in a course required for preservice teachers. Hays studied the impact of assigning a young-adult novel, *If I Ever Get Out of Here* by Onandaga author Eric Gansworth, and using literature circles to discuss and analyze the novel. Hays poses the question: Is exposure to one "authentically authored" novel and the pedagogy of literature circles sufficient to convince preservice teachers of the need for culturally sustaining pedagogy in their own classrooms? (Paris, 2012; McCarty & Lee, 2014) Her findings tell us no. In her words,

"Further work needs to be done in order to move beyond 'scratching the surface' of white privilege and to generate realizations of inequity among preservice teachers."

Finally, Lindsay A. Morcom and Stephanie Roy investigate the impact on academic development of Anishinaabemowin (Ojibwe language) immersion education at the Mnidoo Mnising Anishinaabek Kinoomaage Gamig (MMAK) early learning kindergarten program in Nova Scotia, Canada. Children arrive at MMAK with limited or no knowledge of Anishinaabemowin, and they are exposed to the language for the whole day; the program goal is additive bilingualism, or fluency in both Anishinaabemowin and English. Morcom and Roy report that their "findings reinforce the results of ILI [Indigenous language immersion] research globally; consistently, we find that students may experience some academic or language delay upon starting school in an ILI environment, but that with time these students catch up and may even surpass expectations."

Together, these articles help move us forward to pedagogies that embrace Native linguistic and cultural resources as a central part of schooling. Importantly, as each of the articles shows, these pedagogies have the potential to enrich education for *all* learners. And, they are profoundly important for Native learners.

Warm regards,
Bryan McKinley Jones Brayboy, K. Tsianina Lomawaima,
and Teresa L. McCarty, Editors

REFERENCES

McCarty, T. L., & Lee, T. S. (2014). Critical culturally sustaining/revitalizing pedagogy and Indigenous education sovereignty. *Harvard Educational Review, 84*(1), 101–124.

Paris, D. (2012). Culturally sustaining pedagogy: A needed change in stance, terminology, and practice. *Educational Researcher, 41*(3), 93–97.

Use of Native Language and Culture (NLC) in Elementary and Middle School Instruction as a Predictor of Mathematics Achievement

MARK J. VAN RYZIN AND CLAUDIA G. VINCENT

Because students from American Indian/Alaska Native (AI/AN) backgrounds tend to lag behind their peers in academic achievement, researchers have recommended integrating Native language and culture (NLC) into instruction. However, existing evidence from large-scale studies finds a *negative* effect of the use of NLC on achievement, although this research does not take into account aspects of student background and the learning context. Using a nationally representative dataset, we found that use of NLC had a less negative and/or more positive effect on achievement among students whose families identified more strongly with their Native culture and who were in schools with larger percentages of AI/AN students. Our results support earlier contentions that the use of NLC can be effective in enhancing achievement for at least some AI/AN students; they also suggest that existing approaches to NLC should be expanded to accommodate AI/AN students in a wider range of contexts.

RESEARCH ON AI/AN STUDENTS HAS found that they lag behind their non-AI/AN peers in academic achievement and graduation rates and have higher dropout rates (Aud et al., 2012; Faircloth & Tippeconnic, 2010; National Education Association [NEA], 2010–2011). To improve outcomes for AI/AN students, the research community has recommended that educators integrate Native language and culture (NLC) into instruction (Bishop, Berryman, Cavanagh, & Teddy, 2009; Brayboy & Castagno, 2009; Brayboy, Faircloth, Lee, Maaka, & Richardson, 2015; Castagno & Brayboy, 2008; Chavers, 2000; Martinez, 2014; McCarty & Lee, 2014). Use of NLC in instruction can include, among other things: (a) incorporating Native languages, Native cultural practices, and/or traditional knowledge (Bishop et al., 2009; Brayboy et al., 2015; Brayboy & Castagno, 2009); (b) promoting the presence of Native elders, traditions, and ceremonies in the school (Castagno & Brayboy, 2008; CHiXapkaid et al., 2008; Keeshig-Tobias, 2003; McCarty & Lee, 2014); and, (c) promoting an understanding of the history of tribal self-determination, the impact of institutionalized racism on Native people, and the need for creating change on a systems level (Castagno & Brayboy, 2008; McCarty & Lee, 2014). The research community suggests that schools that integrate these aspects of NLC into instruction may be able to positively impact the behavior and academic performance of AI/AN students (Bishop et al., 2009; Castagno & Brayboy, 2008; Chavers, 2000; Demmert, Towner, & Yap, 2003; McCarty & Lee, 2014; Trujillo & Alston, 2005). This hypothesis is based on qualitative or small-scale studies indicating that AI/AN students are more successful in academic settings that incorporate their language and culture (Apthorp, D'Amato, & Richardson, 2002; August, Goldenberg, & Rueda, 2006; Brayboy & Castagno, 2009; Smallwood, Haynes, & James, 2009).

Existing evidence from multiple large-scale quantitative studies, however, finds a *negative* effect of the use of NLC on student achievement. For example, López, Heilig, and Schram (2013) found that "the more students reported perceiving AI/AN culture was incorporated into instruction, the worse their achievement" (p. 530). They also found that teacher-reported use of NLC had no effect on achievement. Similarly, Jesse, Meyer, and Klute (2014) found negative relationships between student-reported use of NLC and Grades 4 and 8 mathematics and Grade 8 reading achievement (but no effects on Grade 4 reading achievement) and no relationship between teacher-reported use of NLC and student achievement. In addition, they found that school administrator-reported use of NLC was negatively related to Grade 8 reading achievement (but no effects on Grade 4 reading or math achievement or Grade 8 math achievement).

One limitation to this large-scale quantitative research is that it does not take into account important aspects of the learning context, despite evidence that academic achievement among AI/AN populations can be influenced by contextual factors, both in the home and in the school. For example, Powers (2006) found that an individual student's cultural identification moderated the effects of NLC use in the classroom, such that students who identified more closely with their Native culture received more benefit from NLC. This finding was based upon the notion that learning practices used in many Native cultures may not be compatible with the Western approach to education that forms the instructional foundation for most schools—a discontinuity that can contribute to the achievement deficits of AI/AN students. Further, the degree to which AI/AN individuals and families identify with their traditional culture can be expected to vary within a population (Gutiérrez & Rogoff, 2003). Thus, those students whose cultural identity is more closely aligned to traditional beliefs and practices could be expected to gain the most from NLC in schools because their educational experience would more closely align with their cultural traditions (Tyler et al., 2008).

Similarly, Tsethlikai and Rogoff (2013) found that teaching practices that more closely mirrored traditional AI/AN ways of learning, such as attentive involvement in family and community practices and events, were more beneficial to students with a stronger cultural identification. The authors hypothesized that learning through listening may be an especially powerful approach for children whose cultural practices include oral traditions. Here again we encounter the notion of alignment, in which learning practices that incorporate cultural traditions can be more effective and more appealing to AI/AN students (Tsethlikai, 2011).

Achievement of AI/AN students may also be influenced by the cultural context of the school itself. Although the density of AI/AN students in a school has been linked to lower overall achievement (Richards, Vining, & Weimer, 2010), AI/AN density can also be seen as an indicator of the cultural identity of a school (Beaulieu, 2006). Thus, it would be reasonable to hypothesize that use of NLC would be more beneficial in schools with higher AI/AN density and a more Native cultural context.

In this study, we applied these ideas in a quantitative analysis of an existing large-scale dataset. Our research questions (RQs) were:

1. Can cultural identity (as measured by the family's use of Native language in the home and their degree of participation in Native gatherings) moderate the effects of NLC on mathematics achievement?
2. Can the school's cultural context (as measured by the density of AI/AN students in the school) moderate the effects of NLC on mathematics achievement?
3. Can the school's cultural context moderate the effects of cultural identity on the relationship between NLC and mathematics achievement?

Given the results presented by Powers (2006) and Tsethlikai and Rogoff (2013), we hypothesize that cultural identity will serve as a significant moderator, such that students with a stronger cultural identity will be linked to less negative and/or more positive effects of NLC on mathematics achievement (the first research question, or RQ 1). The second and third research questions are exploratory in nature, given the paucity of existing literature, but are included to evaluate (a) whether students in schools with a higher density of AI/AN students will experience greater benefit from NLC in terms of less negative and/or more positive effects on mathematics achievement (RQ 2); and (b) whether schools with a higher density of AI/AN students will enhance or amplify the salutary effect of family context on the link between NLC and mathematics achievement, such that effects of family context are stronger in higher density schools (RQ 3).

To address these research questions, we used data collected by the National Assessment of Educational Progress (NAEP) and the National Indian Education Study (NIES) in 2011. NAEP is an ongoing assessment of students' educational progress and includes assessments of student performance in a range of subject areas including reading, writing, mathematics, science, arts, U.S. history, and geography (see http://nces.ed.gov/nationsreportcard/about/); in this study, we limited our scope to mathematics. In 2011, NAEP conducted national and state assessments in mathematics at Grades 4 and 8 in nationally representative schools.

NIES was carried out during NAEP assessments in Grades 4 and 8 in schools that had one or more AI/AN students who were selected for NAEP. Administered biannually from 2005 to 2011, NIES data collection has now changed to four-year intervals; the 2011 data, therefore, represents the most recent NIES data available (NAEP Grades 4 and 8 reading and math achievement data were released in October 2015, but NIES survey data from 2015 are not yet available). The data collected by NIES included the school survey (completed by school administrators), the teacher survey, and the student survey. Thes surveys provide a number of variables related to the use of NLC in edu ation, such as: (a) the frequency of AI/AN community member visits to schools, (b) the frequency of meetings between school officials and AI/AN community officials and elders, (c) the number of courses about AI/AN traditions and cultures offered by the school, (d) whether instruction in AI/AN language and culture is offered, (e) availability of materials on AI/AN language and culture, (f) teacher use of AI/AN languages during instruction, (g) teacher integration of AI/AN materials into the reading curriculum, and (f) teacher integration of AI/AN materials into the mathematics curriculum. In a previous article, we used exploratory and confirmatory factor analysis to derive a set of statistically defensible constructs to be used in future research on NLC in instruction (Van Ryzin, Vincent, & Hoover, 2016).

Method

Participants

For the analyses in this article, we used NAEP/NIES data from 2011, which consists of about 10,200 AI/AN fourth graders in approximately 1,900 schools and about 10,300 AI/AN eighth graders in approximately 2,000 schools. In addition, the sample includes about 3,000 Grade 4 teachers and 4,600 Grade 8 teachers. For more information, refer to National Center for Education Statistics (2013).

Procedures

The schools and students participating in NAEP assessments are selected to be representative both nationally and at the state level. Samples of schools and students are drawn from each state and from the District of Columbia, and the results are combined to provide accurate estimates of the overall performance of students in the nation and in individual states.

NAEP data collection uses a two-stage sampling procedure. First, a nationally representative sample of schools is selected, then a representative sample of students is selected from the participating schools. To allow detailed examination of AI/AN students' school experiences and performance, Bureau of Indian Education (BIE) schools and AI/AN students are oversampled. All Grade 4 and 8 students who were coded by the school as AI/AN and who participated in an NAEP mathematics, reading, or science assessment were included in the NIES sample and were eligible for participation in the NIES survey (unless the parent exercised the option of not having his or her child answer the NIES questions). Although NIES achievement data are comprised of NAEP mathematics and reading assessments and NIES survey results included AI/AN students who took the NAEP science assessment instead of mathematics or reading, our results were limited to those AI/AN students for whom we had mathematics scores.

Teachers were selected based upon the student sampling procedure; for each sampled student, his/her teacher was requested to fill out the

NIES surveys. There was no explicit sampling of teachers, so teacher data must be considered to be at the student level in multilevel models. Although a teacher can be linked to more than one student, which may create bias in the results, the alternative approach (i.e., creating a teacher level in a multilevel model) is not tenable due to the lack of sampling weights for teachers.

Because NAEP assessments include more questions than any one student could answer, they are designed so that each student takes a randomly selected portion that is representative of the overall assessment. This design allowed for maximum coverage of the content area at Grades 4 and 8 while minimizing the time burden on students.

To collect NIES survey data, the questions were read aloud to all students in Grade 4 who needed assistance (questions were not read aloud to students in Grade 8). Representatives were available to answer any questions that students had as they took the surveys.

Measures

The NAEP Mathematics Framework for Grades 4 and 8, developed by the National Assessment Governing Board, was used to guide the development of the mathematics items. These items focused on five mathematics content areas: number properties and operations, measurement, geometry, data analysis, statistics and probability, and algebra (Grade 8 only).

Proficiencies in these content areas were summarized through Item Response Theory (IRT) models. Proficiency values, or "plausible values," were drawn at random from a conditional distribution for each NAEP respondent, given his or her response to a subset of mathematics items and a specified group of background variables. These plausible values are considered to be estimates of how a student would have scored if he/she had actually completed every item in the assessment. The plausible values for each content area were combined to generate a set of overall plausible values for mathematics, and these were used as the outcome variables for our analyses.

NIES student, teacher, and administrator surveys were developed by a technical review panel including Native scholars. From these items, we used exploratory and confirmatory factor analysis to derive the following set of constructs representing use of NLC in the classroom (see Van Ryzin et al., 2016, for details). The creation of composite variables to represent each aspect of NLC was necessary given the complexity of the models and the analysis framework (Hierarchical Linear Modeling

[HLM]) we selected; see Analysis Plan in the next section. Following are the individual constructs we used in our analysis.

Live exposure (student-report). In the fourth grade, this variable measured the degree to which students were given live access to AI/AN traditions and culture in the classroom through use of language (item 4), school visitors (item 5), and field trips (item 6). Items 5 and 6 were reverse coded so that higher scores indicated more access. Since the items were on different scales (yes/no versus 3- or 4-item Likert scales), all items were standardized; the standardized items were then averaged to form a single composite.

In the eighth grade, this variable measured the degree to which students were given live access to AI/AN culture in the classroom through presentations on Native traditions and customs (item 6a), arts and crafts demonstrations (item 6b), music and dance (item 6c), and field trips to museums or Native communities (item 6d). All items were reverse coded to ensure that higher scores indicated more exposure. Items were on the same scale and were averaged to form a single composite.

Media exposure (student-report). In the fourth grade, this variable measured the degree to which students were exposed to learning materials with AI/AN themes (items 7, 8, and 12). Items 7 and 8 were reverse coded so that higher scores indicated more access. Since the items were on different scales (yes/no versus 3-item Likert scale), all items were standardized; the standardized items were then averaged to form a single composite.

In the eighth grade, this variable included items 7a–b and 8a–b. All items were reverse coded to ensure that higher scores indicated more exposure. Items were on the same scale and were averaged to form a single composite.

Teacher preparation (teacher-report). For teachers of fourth-grade students, this variable measured the degree to which teachers made use of available resources and professional development opportunities in order to improve their teaching and, in turn, the academic performance of their AI/AN students (items 5a–e and 6). Items were on the same scale and were averaged to form a single composite. For teachers of eighth-grade students, this variable was created in an identical manner but used items 4a–e and 6 instead of items 5a–e and 6.

Math instruction (teacher-report). For teachers of fourth-grade students, this variable measured the degree to which teachers incorporated AI/AN culture and history into their mathematics instruction (items 9, 16, 17, and 18a–d). Since the items were on different scales (4-item versus 5-item Likert scales), all items were standardized; the standardized items were then averaged to form a single composite.

For teachers of eighth-grade students, this variable was created in an identical manner but used items 19, 20, 21, and 22a–d instead of items 9, 16, 17, and 18a–d. Since the items were on different scales (4-item versus 5-item Likert scales), all items were standardized; the standardized items were then averaged to form a single composite.

Local involvement (administrator-report). This variable measured the degree to which school administrators for fourth-grade students involved local representatives of AI/AN tribes in their school (items 9a–c, 10a–b). Items were on the same scale and were averaged to form a single composite. For eighth grade, this variable was created in an identical manner.

Cultural instruction (administrator-report). This variable measured the extent to which administrators for fourth-grade students believed that students in their school received instruction in Native history, traditions, arts, and tribal government (items 14c–f). Items were on the same scale and were averaged to form a single composite. For eighth grade, this variable was created in an identical manner.

Family/school context. We used two variables independently to indicate the family cultural context: the degree to which the family spoke a Native language in the home (1 = never or hardly ever, 2 = once or twice a month, 3 = once or twice a week, 4 = every day or almost); and, the frequency with which the family attended Native ceremonies and gatherings (1 = never, 2 = every few years, 3 = at least once a year, 4 = several times a year). The school context was indicated by a single variable representing the percentage of AI/AN students in the school.

Student covariates. We controlled for factors that could be expected to predict math achievement including: whether the student was eligible for free or reduced-price lunch (0 = no, 1 = yes); whether the student was classified as an English language learner (ELL; 0 = no, 1 = yes); whether the student had an Individual Education Plan (IEP;

0=no, 1=yes); and the students' self-rating in math (1=poor, 2=average, 3=good, 4=very good).

Analysis Plan

We conducted the analyses using HLM, which supports the use of plausible values as outcomes. Since NAEP used five plausible values for mathematics achievement, HLM performed each analysis five times and then aggregated the results, adjusting the standard errors to reflect the variance in the regression coefficients across the five sets of results. HLM also supports the use of weighting at each level, which was required in our analysis due to the school and student sampling mechanism in NAEP/ NIES. We used a two-level model, with students at level one nested within schools at level two. As discussed earlier, a separate level for teachers, which would imply a three-level model with students nested within teachers nested within schools, was not possible given that teachers were not deliberately sampled, and thus no weighting variable for teachers was provided in the dataset.

To test whether the effects of NLC were moderated by family and school context, we used interaction terms. For RQ 1, to test the interaction between NLC (e.g., student-report live exposure) and the family context (e.g., frequency of Native language spoken in the home), we multiplied these variables together to form an interaction term and then included the interaction term in the model along with the main effects (i.e., the variables themselves). If this interaction term was statistically significant, it would indicate that the effect of NLC on mathematics achievement varied across the levels of family context (e.g., from low to high frequency of Native language spoken in the home).

To test whether school-level percentage of AI/AN students moderated the effects of student- or teacher-report NLC (which is part of RQ 2), cross-level interactions were created in HLM. To evaluate the potential for the school context to moderate the effect of family context on the link between NLC and instruction (RQ 3), we used three-way interactions, which are conceptually similar to two-way interactions (e.g., between family context and NLC) but with an added third variable (e.g., school context). As is standard practice, we included all relevant main effects in the model when testing interactions. Grand-mean centering for all variables was used, meaning that variables without meaningful zero values were averaged across the entire sample; this ensures that the intercept values from the models are interpretable as the scores for the average student. Random effects for each level one predictor were tested and discarded if they were not significant; these effects enable HLM to model differences among students within schools.

We conducted three sets of analyses for both fourth and eighth grade; in each case, we first explored the effects of teacher-report NLC, then student-report, then administrator-report, and we controlled for key covariates in each model, such as ELL or special education status. In each set of models, we first evaluated main effects for NLC (Model 1), then we explored moderation by family context (Models 2a and 2b, corresponding to RQ 1), and finally we explored moderation by family and school context simultaneously (Models 3a and 3b, corresponding to RQ 2 and 3). The following is a sample model that evaluates moderation of the live exposure aspect of student-report NLC by both family and school context:

(level one—student) $\text{Math}_{ij} = \pi_{0j} + \pi_{1j} \text{ (live exposure)}_{ij} + \pi_{2j} \text{ (family context)}_{ij} + \pi_{3j} \text{ (interaction)}_{ij} + \pi_{4j} \text{ (student covariate)}_{ij} + e_{ij}$

(level two—school) $\pi_{0j} = \beta_{00} + \beta_{01} \text{ (percent Native students)}_j + r_{0j}$
(level two—school) $\pi_{1j} = \beta_{10} + \beta_{11} \text{ (percent Native students)}_j + r_{1j}$
(level two—school) $\pi_{2j} = \beta_{20} + \beta_{21} \text{ (percent Native students)}_j + r_{2j}$
(level two—school) $\pi_{3j} = \beta_{30} + \beta_{31} \text{ (percent Native students)}_j + r_{3j}$
(level two—school) $\pi_{4j} = \beta_{40} + r_{4j}$

In this model, the regression coefficients (βs) are interpreted in terms of their effects on the outcome variable (i.e., mathematics achievement) and have the following interpretation:

β_{00}: the regression intercept
β_{01}: the main effect for the school's percent Native students (i.e., density)
β_{10}: the main effect for live exposure
β_{11}: the interaction between live exposure and percent Native students (RQ 2)
β_{20}: the main effect for family context
β_{21}: the interaction between family context and percent Native students
β_{30}: the interaction between live exposure and family context (RQ 1)
β_{31}: the interaction between live exposure, family context, and percent Native students (RQ 3)
β_{40}: the main effect for a student covariate (e.g., ELL; no interaction with percent Native students was tested)

Results

Descriptive data are presented in Table 1. In each of our results tables (Tables 2 and 4 through 8), Model 1 evaluates the main effects of NLC (to serve as a comparison with previous research), Models 2a and 2b refer to moderation of NLC by family context (RQ 1), and Models 3a and 3b add a consideration of school context (RQs 2 and 3). We present the key regression coefficients in the following text to aid the reader's interpretation of the tables.

We present the results from teacher-report NLC predicting fourth-grade math achievement in Table 2. Unlike previous results that found no effects for teacher-report of NLC (Jesse et al., 2014), we find significant negative effects for teacher use of Native materials in preparation

Table 1. Descriptive Data

	Grade 4 (N=4500)		Grade 8 (N=3300)	
Level 1 (students)	Mean	SD	Mean	SD
School lunch eligibility	.80	.40	.75	.43
Student classified as ELL	.16	.36	.12	.32
Student has an IEP	.15	.35	.13	.33
Math self-rating	3.40	1.43	2.56	.90
Family speaks Native language	2.22	1.28	2.24	1.29
Family attends Native gatherings	2.37	1.21	2.71	1.18
Live exposure (student-report)	.00	.66	1.85	.68
Media exposure (student-report)	.00	.72	.45	.36
Teacher preparation (teacher-report)	2.26	.85	2.12	.84
Math instruction (teacher-report)	.00	.81	.00	.79
	Grade 4 (N=1200)		Grade 8 (N=1000)	
Level 2 (schools)	Mean	SD	Mean	SD
Percent AI/AN students	23.39	34.87	23.79	35.25
Local involvement (admin-report)	1.57	.60	1.59	.65
Cultural instruction (admin-report)	.68	.32	.62	.38

Table 2. Results Predicting Math Achievement in Grade 4 Using Teacher Reports of NLC (unstandardized coefficients and standard errors)

	Model 1	Model 2a	Model 2b
Level 1 (students)			
School lunch eligibility	−11.24*** (1.15)	−10.69*** (1.19)	−10.90*** (1.17)
Student classified as ELL	−18.42*** (2.63)	−17.08*** (2.51)	−17.72*** (2.63)
Student has an IEP	−23.52*** (1.66)	−23.49*** (1.74)	−23.14*** (1.66)
Math self-rating	6.35*** (.78)	6.27*** (.73)	6.19*** (.74)
Family speaks Native language	−1.77* (.71)	−1.53* (.77)	−1.27 (.71)
Family attends Native gatherings	−.71 (.46)	−.73 (.50)	−.49 (.49)
Teacher preparation (teacher-report)	−4.19* (1.22)	−5.24** (1.37)	−4.43 (1.41)
Math instruction (teacher-report)	−1.36 (1.44)	−.78 (1.58)	−1.86 (1.49)
Interaction (prep * language)	–	1.89* (.73)	–
Interaction (prep * gatherings)	–	−.11 (.58)	–
Interaction (math * language)	–	–	2.67** (.82)
Interaction (math * gatherings)	–	–	1.38* (.70)
Level 2 (schools)	–	–	–

	Model 3a	Model 3b
Level 1 (students)		
School lunch eligibility	−9.39*** (1.17)	−9.48*** (1.15)
Student classified as ELL	−16.59*** (2.62)	−16.94*** (2.67)
Student has an IEP	−23.04*** (1.64)	−23.35*** (1.65)
Math self-rating	6.28*** (.73)	6.37*** (.76)
Family speaks Native language	−2.31* (.99)	−2.84* (1.04)
Family attends Native gatherings	−1.85 (1.62)	−1.29 (1.18)
Teacher preparation (teacher-report)	−3.14 (1.60)	−3.31 (1.52)

(continued)

Table 2 *(continued)*

	Model 3a	Model 3b
Math instruction (teacher-report)	−.35 (1.37)	−1.48 (2.11)
Interaction (prep * language)	.39 (.85)	–
Interaction (prep * gatherings)	−1.32 (.89)	–
Interaction (math * language)	–	−2.11 (1.85)
Interaction (math * gatherings)	–	−.64 (1.87)
Level 2 (schools)		
Percent AI/AN students	−.12*** (.03)	−.10*** (.03)
Interaction (percent * language)	.04* (.02)	.06* (.02)
Interaction (percent * gatherings)	.03 (.02)	.02 (.02)
Interaction (percent * prep)	.05* (.03)	–
Interaction (percent * prep * language)	−.03 (.02)	–
Interaction (percent * prep * gatherings)	.02 (.02)	–
Interaction (percent * math)	–	.00 (.03)
Interaction (percent * math * language)	–	.06* (.03)
Interaction (percent * math * gatherings)	–	.03 (.03)

*$p < .05$. **$p < .01$. ***$p < .001$.

($B = -4.19^*$) but not for the use of Native concepts in math instruction ($B = -1.36$; see Model 1). In Models 2a and 2b, the significant interaction terms suggest that both aspects of NLC are moderated by the family context; specifically, both depend on the degree to which the family speaks a Native language ($B = 1.89^*$ and $B = 2.67^{**}$), and the impact of NLC in math instruction on student math achievement also depends on the degree to which the family attends Native ceremonies and gatherings ($B = 1.38^*$). The magnitude and positive sign of these interaction terms suggest that students from families who speak a Native language and/or often attend a Native gathering may experience a less negative and/or more positive effect for teacher-report NLC as compared to other students. In Model 3a, the significant interaction term ($B = .05^*$) suggests that students in schools with higher percentages of AI/AN students will experience less negative and/or more positive effects from teacher use of Native materials in preparation; the three-way interactions were not significant. In Model 3b, the significant three-way interaction ($B = .06^*$) suggests that students whose families speak Native language more often will experience a less negative and/or more positive effect of NLC on achievement, and that this effect is amplified for students in schools with higher percentages of AI/AN students. Finally, the student covariates all had significant effects in the expected directions (e.g., the presence of an IEP had a negative effect). This aspect of our results was consistent across all analyses.

To aid the understanding of these interaction terms, we provide a set of predicted effects for both aspects of teacher-reported NLC in different contexts in Table 3. The first number in each column represents the "main" effect, or the overall effect of each aspect of NLC for the entire sample. The next four numbers represent the effect of NLC for students whose families have varying degrees of identification with Native culture. As the numbers suggest, the effects of NLC become more positive as students' families report a greater degree of Native identification. Following this, we provide three sets of numbers to document how those families would perform in schools that were mostly non-AI/AN (only 5% AI/AN), evenly split between AI/AN and non-AI/AN (50% AI/AN), and mostly AI/AN (95% AI/AN)[1]. As discussed earlier, the effects of teacher-reported NLC across the range of family cultural identification becomes less negative and/or more positive as the AI/AN density increases.

In Table 4, we present the results from student-reported NLC predicting fourth-grade math achievement. In Model 1, we found a significant negative effect for live exposure ($B = -7.02^{***}$), which echoes previous work (e.g., Jesse et al., 2014); media exposure had no significant effect. In Model 2a, we find that the negative effect for live exposure is moderated by the degree to which the family speaks a Native language ($B = 4.04^{**}$); the magnitude and positive sign of the interaction term suggests that students from families who speak a Native language often may experience a less negative and/or more positive effect for student-reported NLC as compared to students from families who don't speak a Native language at home (in Model 2b, we find no moderating

Table 3. Main and Moderated Effects of Teacher-Report NLC on Grade 4 Math Achievement

	Teacher preparation	*Math instruction*
Main effect (Model 1)	–4.19	–1.36
Moderated effect—Family context		
Never/rarely (speak Native language)	–6.91	–5.51
Sometimes (speak Native language)	–5.43	–2.27
Often (speak Native language)	–3.92	.98
All the time (speak Native language)	–2.41	4.22
Moderated effect—Family and school context		
Mostly non–AI/AN school (5% AI/AN students)		
Never/rarely (speak Native language)	–3.24	–1.75
Sometimes (speak Native language)	–2.93	–1.51
Often (speak Native language)	–2.62	–1.27
All the time (speak Native language)	–2.31	–1.03
Evenly split school (50% AI/AN students)		
Never/rarely (speak Native language)	–.99	–4.18
Sometimes (speak Native language)	–.68	–1.78
Often (speak Native language)	–.37	.62
All the time (speak Native language)	–.06	3.02
Mostly AI/AN school (95% AI/AN students)		
Never/rarely (speak Native language)	1.26	–6.61
Sometimes (speak Native language)	1.57	–2.05
Often (speak Native language)	1.88	2.51
All the time (speak Native language)	2.20	7.07

effects for media exposure). In Model 3a, there is a significant three-way interaction between live exposure, frequency of attending Native gatherings, and percent AI/AN students in the school ($B = .04^*$); the positive sign of the interaction term suggests that students whose families attend Native gatherings more frequently will experience a less negative and/or more positive effect of NLC on achievement and that this effect is amplified for students in schools with higher percentages of AI/AN students. In Model 3b, we find a significant interaction between media exposure and percent AI/AN students ($B = .05^*$), suggesting that this aspect of NLC is more effective in schools with higher AI/AN density.

Table 5 contains the results for administrator-reported use of NLC. As in previous research (e.g., Jesse et al., 2014), Model 1 suggests

Table 4. Results Predicting Math Achievement in Grade 4 Using Student Reports of NLC (unstandardized coefficients and standard errors)

	Model 1	Model 2a	Model 2b
Level 1 (students)			
School lunch eligibility	−11.76*** (1.18)	−11.07*** (1.17)	−11.80*** (1.17)
Student classified as ELL	−18.33*** (2.35)	−17.32*** (2.24)	−18.34*** (2.35)
Student has an IEP	−23.10*** (1.34)	−23.12*** (1.34)	−23.15*** (1.35)
Math self-rating	6.40*** (.73)	6.25*** (.72)	6.38*** (.73)
Family speaks Native language	−.69 (.46)	−1.31 (.76)	−.60 (.69)
Family attends Native gatherings	−.48 (.44)	−.42 (.45)	−.43 (.89)
Live exposure (student-report)	−7.02*** (1.04)	−6.80*** (1.65)	−7.03*** (1.04)
Media exposure (student-report)	−.24 (.80)	−.57 (1.28)	−.61 (.81)
Interaction (live * language)	–	4.04** (1.56)	–
Interaction (live * gatherings)	–	−.40 (1.36)	–
Interaction (media * language)	–	–	−.93 (.81)
Interaction (media * gatherings)	–	–	−1.05 (.74)
Level 2 (schools)	–	–	–

	Model 3a	Model 3b
Level 1 (students)		
School lunch eligibility	−9.97*** (1.13)	−10.10*** (1.13)
Student classified as ELL	−16.31*** (2.33)	−15.90*** (2.26)
Student has an IEP	−23.33*** (1.35)	−23.43*** (1.39)
Math self-rating	6.32*** (.73)	6.33*** (.73)
Family speaks Native language	−1.26 (.67)	−1.50 (.90)
Family attends Native gatherings	−1.18 (.70)	−.48 (.98)
Live exposure (student-report)	−5.20*** (1.09)	−6.11*** (1.08)
Media exposure (student-report)	−.54 (.78)	−2.34* (.92)

(continued)

Table 4 *(continued)*

	Model 3a	Model 3b
Interaction (live * language)	3.90** (.99)	–
Interaction (live * gatherings)	–2.41 (1.85)	–
Interaction (media * language)	–	–2.20 (1.19)
Interaction (media * gatherings)	–	–1.64 (.85)
Level 2 (schools)		
Percent AI/AN students	–.12*** (.02)	–.12*** (.02)
Interaction (percent * language)	.03* (.01)	.04* (.01)
Interaction (percent * gatherings)	.04* (.02)	.03 (.02)
Interaction (percent * live)	–.03 (.02)	–
Interaction (percent * live * language)	–.03 (.02)	–
Interaction (percent * live * gatherings)	.04* (.02)	–
Interaction (percent * media)	–	.05* (.02)
Interaction (percent * media * language)	–	.02 (.02)
Interaction (percent * media * gatherings)	–	.02 (.02)

*$p<.05$. **$p<.01$. ***$p<.001$.

that local involvement has a negative effect on math achievement ($B=-8.10$***); cultural instruction had no effect. Model 2a suggests that this effect is moderated by the degree to which the family speaks a Native language ($B=1.66$*). As with both student- and teacher-reported NLC, the magnitude and positive sign of the interaction term suggests that students from families who speak a Native language often may experience a less negative and/or more positive effect for local involvement, whereas students from families who don't speak a Native language often would experience a more negative effect (there were no moderating effects for cultural instruction). In Models 3a and 3b, we find no moderating effects for AI/AN density on administrator-reported use of NLC, but we do find a significant positive interaction between

Table 5. Results Predicting Math Achievement in Grade 4 Using Administrator Reports of NLC (unstandardized coefficients and standard errors)

	Model 1	Model 2a	Model 2b
Level 1 (students)			
School lunch eligibility	−11.16*** (1.15)	−10.95*** (1.13)	−11.12*** (1.15)
Student classified as ELL	−18.77*** (2.33)	−18.78*** (2.34)	−18.78*** (2.32)
Student has an IEP	−24.44*** (1.37)	−24.04*** (1.35)	−24.35*** (1.38)
Math self-rating	6.06*** (.75)	6.10*** (.76)	6.04*** (.74)
Family speaks Native language	−1.36* (.66)	−1.99** (.74)	−1.41* (.66)
Family attends Native gatherings	−.51 (.83)	−.03 (.84)	−.51 (.88)
Level 2 (schools)			
Local involvement (admin-report)	−8.10*** (1.37)	−7.91*** (1.40)	−8.07*** (1.36)
Cultural instruction (admin-report)	.74 (2.81)	.63 (2.81)	.91 (3.01)
Interaction (local * language)	–	1.66* (.63)	–
Interaction (local * gatherings)	–	−1.39 (1.36)	–
Interaction (cultural * language)	–	–	1.11 (1.30)
Interaction (cultural * gatherings)	–	–	−.07 (1.43)

	Model 3a	Model 3b
Level 1 (students)		
School lunch eligibility	−9.88*** (1.11)	−9.92*** (1.13)
Student classified as ELL	−17.09*** (2.33)	−17.17*** (2.28)
Student has an IEP	−24.14*** (1.36)	−24.44*** (1.41)
Math self-rating	6.14*** (.74)	6.06*** (.73)
Family speaks Native language	−2.27* (.89)	−2.36** (.87)
Family attends Native gatherings	−.38 (.97)	−.73 (1.04)
Level 2 (schools)		
Local involvement (admin-report)	−3.78 (2.06)	−3.54 (1.91)

(continued)

Table 5 *(continued)*

	Model 3a	Model 3b
Cultural instruction (admin-report)	1.40 (2.60)	−.01 (3.02)
Interaction (local * language)	.29 (1.17)	−
Interaction (local * gatherings)	−3.09 (2.21)	−
Interaction (cultural * language)	−	−.40 (1.72)
Interaction (cultural * gatherings)	−	−.12 (1.42)
Percent AI/AN students	−.13*** (.03)	−.10*** (.03)
Interaction (language * percent)	.03 (.02)	.03 (.02)
Interaction (gatherings * percent)	.03* (.02)	.02 (.02)
Interaction (local * percent)	.07 (1.13)	−
Interaction (local * percent * language)	.15 (.51)	−
Interaction (local * percent * gatherings)	.27 (.50)	−
Interaction (cultural * percent)	−	−1.64 (.99)
Interaction (cultural * percent * language)	−	.66 (.49)
Interaction (cultural * percent * gatherings)	−	−.45 (.45)

*$p < .05$. **$p < .01$. ***$p < .001$.

the degree to which the family attends Native gatherings and percent AI/AN students in the school ($B = .03^*$; see Model 3a), suggesting that students who attend Native gatherings more often score higher in mathematics achievement in schools with greater AI/AN density.

In the next set of analyses, we examined effects of NLC on eighth-grade mathematics achievement. In Table 6, we find results similar to those reported earlier for teacher-reported NLC, that is, a negative effect for teacher-reported use of Native materials for preparation ($B = -5.48^{***}$) but no significant effect for use of Native concepts in

Table 6. Results Predicting Math Achievement in Grade 8 Using Teacher Reports of NLC (unstandardized coefficients and standard errors)

	Model 1	Model 2a	Model 2b
Level 1 (students)			
School lunch eligibility	−10.19*** (1.91)	−10.12*** (1.94)	−10.39*** (1.86)
Student classified as ELL	−19.84*** (3.13)	−19.76*** (3.20)	−19.06*** (3.16)
Student has an IEP	−29.37*** (2.15)	−28.94*** (2.16)	−28.95*** (2.23)
Math self-rating	12.80*** (.71)	12.78*** (.70)	12.66*** (.87)
Family speaks Native language	−3.33*** (.89)	−3.63*** (.89)	−3.51** (.87)
Family attends Native gatherings	−1.39 (.98)	−1.02 (.90)	−.73 (1.07)
Teacher preparation (teacher-report)	−5.48*** (1.43)	−5.47*** (1.49)	−5.94** (1.56)
Math instruction (teacher-report)	−.73 (1.49)	−.77 (1.74)	−.29 (1.67)
Interaction (prep * language)	–	−.85 (.97)	–
Interaction (prep * gatherings)	–	1.67* (.80)	–
Interaction (math * language)	–	–	.52 (1.45)
Interaction (math * gatherings)	–	–	2.84† (1.42)
Level 2 (schools)	–	–	–

	Model 3a	Model 3b
Level 1 (students)		
School lunch eligibility	−9.72*** (2.03)	−9.86*** (1.98)
Student classified as ELL	−19.85*** (3.16)	−18.84*** (3.19)
Student has an IEP	−28.34*** (2.10)	−28.99*** (2.14)
Math self-rating	12.63*** (.70)	12.80*** (.72)
Family speaks Native language	−4.23** (1.27)	−4.92*** (1.27)
Family attends Native gatherings	−2.25 (1.36)	−.64 (1.48)
Teacher preparation (teacher-report)	−6.38*** (1.81)	−4.90** (1.50)

(continued)

Table 6 *(continued)*

	Model 3a	Model 3b
Math instruction (teacher-report)	−1.49 (2.50)	−.69 (2.77)
Interaction (prep * language)	−1.92 (1.33)	–
Interaction (prep * gatherings)	.19 (1.08)	–
Interaction (math * language)	–	−3.61 (3.00)
Interaction (math * gatherings)	–	3.03 (2.24)
Level 2 (schools)		
Percent AI/AN students	−.04 (.04)	−.03 (.03)
Interaction (percent * language)	.02 (.02)	.02 (.02)
Interaction (percent * gatherings)	.04 (.02)	.03 (.03)
Interaction (percent * prep)	.02 (.04)	–
Interaction (percent * prep * language)	.07* (.03)	–
Interaction (percent * prep * gatherings)	.02 (.02)	–
Interaction (percent * math)	–	−.02 (.05)
Interaction (percent * math * language)	–	.09* (.04)
Interaction (percent * math * gatherings)	–	−.05 (.03)

†$p = .05$. *$p < .05$. **$p < .01$. ***$p < .001$.

math instruction (see Model 1). Interestingly, we also see a significant and negative main effect for use of Native language in the home ($B = -3.33$***), suggesting that students who speak Native language in the home more often may score lower on the achievement tests. As with previous results, we found a significant positive interaction term for the family context, such that students whose families attend Native gatherings more often may experience a less negative and/or more positive effect for teacher preparation ($B = 1.67$*; see Model 2a); the parallel effect in Model 2b (i.e., use of NLC in math instruction) was close to

Table 7. Results Predicting Math Achievement in Grade 8 Using Student Reports of NLC (unstandardized coefficients and standard errors)

	Model 1	Model 2a	Model 2b
Level 1 (students)			
School lunch eligibility	−10.41*** (1.45)	−10.42*** (1.47)	−10.30*** (1.46)
Student classified as ELL	−21.31*** (3.40)	−20.80*** (3.26)	−20.70*** (3.26)
Student has an IEP	−30.80*** (2.01)	−30.77*** (2.01)	−30.86*** (1.98)
Math self-rating	12.08*** (.80)	12.18*** (.82)	12.20*** (.82)
Family speaks Native language	−3.07*** (.60)	−2.61** (.80)	−2.57** (.82)
Family attends Native gatherings	−1.41 (.80)	−.97 (.94)	−1.01 (.98)
Live exposure (student-report)	−4.54*** (.97)	−4.79*** (1.09)	−5.10*** (1.05)
Media exposure (student-report)	−10.05*** (1.87)	−9.44*** (2.08)	−8.94*** (2.11)
Interaction (live * language)	–	.19 (.72)	–
Interaction (live * gatherings)	–	.83 (.68)	–
Interaction (media * language)	–	–	.46 (.79)
Interaction (media * gatherings)	–	–	.45 (.72)
Level 2 (schools)	–	–	–

	Model 3a	Model 3b
Level 1 (students)		
School lunch eligibility	−9.78*** (1.57)	−9.79*** (1.56)
Student classified as ELL	−19.29*** (3.26)	−19.04*** (3.24)
Student has an IEP	−31.00*** (2.00)	−31.01*** (2.00)
Math self-rating	12.13*** (.82)	12.22*** (.81)
Family speaks Native language	−2.56* (1.00)	−2.39* (1.12)
Family attends Native gatherings	−1.18 (1.04)	−1.64 (1.18)
Live exposure (student-report)	−4.83*** (1.36)	−3.75** (1.24)
Media exposure (student-report)	−8.01*** (2.16)	−8.44*** (2.44)

(continued)

Table 7 *(continued)*

	Model 3a	Model 3b
Interaction (live * language)	−.46 (1.03)	−
Interaction (live * gatherings)	.63 (.89)	−
Interaction (media * language)	−	.34 (1.08)
Interaction (media * gatherings)	−	.07 (.83)
Level 2 (schools)		
Percent AI/AN students	−.07* (.03)	−.06* (.03)
Interaction (percent * language)	.00 (.02)	.00 (.02)
Interaction (percent * gatherings)	.04* (.02)	.04* (.02)
Interaction (percent * live)	.08* (.03)	−
Interaction (percent * live * language)	.01 (.02)	−
Interaction (percent * live * gatherings)	−.02 (.02)	−
Interaction (percent * media)	−	−.10 (.07)
Interaction (percent * media * language)	−	.01 (.02)
Interaction (percent * media * gatherings)	−	.01 (.02)

*$p < .05$. **$p < .01$. ***$p < .001$.

significance ($B = 2.84$; $p = .05$). Finally, again mirroring our previous results, we find that these relationships are moderated by the school context, with students whose families spoke Native language in the home more often experiencing less negative and/or more positive effects in schools with higher percentages of AI/AN students ($B = .07*$ and $B = .09*$; see Models 3a and 3b).

In Table 7, we find significant negative effects for both live exposure and media access ($B = −4.54***$ and $B = −10.05***$; see Model 1). In Models 2a and 2b, we find no significant interaction with the family context, but in Model 3a we do find a significant interaction between live exposure and

Table 8. Results Predicting Math Achievement in Grade 8 Using Administrator Reports of NLC (unstandardized coefficients and standard errors)

	Model 1	Model 2a	Model 2b
Level 1 (students)			
School lunch eligibility	−11.11*** (1.43)	−10.72*** (1.52)	−10.84*** (1.51)
Student classified as ELL	−20.97*** (3.16)	−19.76*** (3.14)	−19.88*** (2.94)
Student has an IEP	−31.88*** (1.97)	−31.54*** (1.94)	−31.84*** (1.95)
Math self-rating	11.91*** (.79)	12.13*** (.73)	12.11*** (.85)
Family speaks Native language	−3.09*** (.78)	−2.99** (.94)	−3.16*** (.82)
Family attends Native gatherings	−1.39 (.95)	−1.57 (1.05)	−1.37 (.99)
Level 2 (schools)			
Local involvement (admin-report)	−6.67** (1.69)	−6.72** (1.72)	−6.93** (1.72)
Cultural instruction (admin-report)	−2.64 (2.36)	−2.82 (2.43)	−1.89 (2.48)
Interaction (local * language)	–	−.57 (.86)	–
Interaction (local * gatherings)	–	1.25 (.83)	–
Interaction (cultural * language)	–	–	−.71 (1.59)
Interaction (cultural * gatherings)	–	–	2.61 (1.60)

	Model 3a	Model 3b
Level 1 (students)		
School lunch eligibility	−10.68*** (1.56)	−10.96*** (1.52)
Student classified as ELL	−16.84*** (3.80)	−16.99*** (3.69)
Student has an IEP	−30.27*** (2.16)	−30.56*** (2.16)
Math self-rating	11.41*** (.90)	10.49*** (.88)
Family speaks Native language	−2.84* (1.89)	−3.03** (1.08)
Family attends Native gatherings	−1.69 (1.15)	−1.89 (1.11)
Level 2 (schools)		
Local involvement (admin-report)	−5.95* (2.46)	−5.43* (2.35)

(continued)

Table 8 *(continued)*

	Model 3a	*Model 3b*
Cultural instruction (admin-report)	−2.65 (3.16)	−2.32 (3.45)
Interaction (local * language)	−.58 (1.78)	−
Interaction (local * gatherings)	−.83 (1.53)	−
Interaction (cultural * language)	−	−.70 (1.87)
Interaction (cultural * gatherings)	−	.57 (1.78)
Percent AI/AN students	−.06 (.04)	−.08* (.04)
Interaction (language * percent)	.01 (.02)	.01 (.02)
Interaction (gatherings * percent)	.01 (.02)	.01 (.02)
Interaction (local * percent)	.22 (.89)	−
Interaction (local * percent * language)	−.11 (.71)	−
Interaction (local * percent * gatherings)	1.21† (.61)	−
Interaction (cultural * percent)	−	1.58 (.97)
Interaction (cultural * percent * language)	−	−.30 (.83)
Interaction (cultural * percent * gatherings)	−	1.76* (.74)

†$p = .05$. *$p < .05$. **$p < .01$. ***$p < .001$.

AI/AN density ($B = .08*$), suggesting that the effect of live access is less negative and/or more positive in schools with greater percentages of AI/AN students; however, the effect of media access is not moderated (see Model 3b).

Finally, in Table 8, we find that administrator-report of local Native involvement has a negative effect on math achievement ($B = −6.67**$), but cultural instruction does not (see Model 1). In Models 2a and 2b, we find no significant interaction with the family context, but in Models 3a and 3b, we do find interaction terms suggesting that the effects of both aspects of administrator-report NLC are less negative and/or more positive for students whose families attend Native gatherings more often; these effects are amplified for students in schools with greater percentages of AI/AN students ($B = 1.21$, $p = .05$; and $B = 1.76^*$).

Discussion

Previous large-scale research exploring the use of NLC on academic achievement has found negative effects (Jesse et al., 2014; López et al., 2013), which directly contradicts much of the theory and small-scale research supporting the use of NLC in schools (August et al., 2006; Brayboy et al., 2015; McCarty & Lee, 2014; Smallwood et al., 2009). In this study, we find that a student's family context can moderate these negative links, at least with regard to math achievement; both the degree to which the family spoke a Native language in the home and the frequency with which the family attended native gatherings emerged as moderators. As argued by Powers (2006), we can understand these findings in terms of cultural alignment between home and school: students whose cultural identity is more aligned to traditional Native beliefs and activities should gain the most from Native-focused educational programs.

There were also significant effects related to the school context, and these effects suggested that, in many cases, the school context amplified the moderating impact of the family cultural context such that NLC was most successful with students who possessed the strongest Native cultural identification and who attended schools with the highest percentages of AI/AN students. These findings suggest that greater cultural alignment between home and school can be beneficial for AI/AN students. There were also suggestions that the school context may moderate the use of NLC directly, as with the significant two-way interaction with student-reported NLC (see Table 7, Model 3a; $B = .04^*$).

Our analysis also produced some interesting results unrelated to NLC. For example, in Table 5, Model 3a contained a significant interaction effect between the family and school context ($B = .03^*$), suggesting that students whose families attended Native gatherings with more frequency had higher test scores when they attended schools with higher percentages of AI/AN students. These results stand in contrast with previous research that found a negative effect for AI/AN density (Richards et al., 2010) and again emphasized the importance of cultural alignment between the home and school in terms of promoting the achievement of AI/AN students.

If we are to acknowledge that use of NLC may be more effective for AI/AN students whose family and school contexts reflect more Native-centric cultural identification, then we must also consider that NLC may be less effective, or perhaps even detrimental, to AI/AN students whose cultural identification is less Native-centric and/or who are in schools with lower AI/AN density. One possible explanation for this phenomenon is the theory of *stereotype threat*, which states that students from ethnic minorities may score lower when negative stereotypes regarding their ethnicity are more salient (Fryberg, Markus, Oyserman, & Stone, 2008; Steele & Aronson, 1995). Stereotypes regarding AI/AN students are likely to be more salient in schools with lower AI/AN densities, which is precisely the situation where, our results suggest, students will be more negatively impacted by the use of NLC. For AI/AN students in mostly non-Native schools, the use of NLC may represent a reminder of their own Native heritage, which may create a context of lowered expectations and/or pressure to perform that contributes to more negative outcomes.

This hypothesis may also explain why the results from NAEP/NIES, indicating negative overall effects for NLC, have been at variance with previous research that generally finds a positive effect for NLC. Specifically, NAEP/NIES contain results from AI/AN students in a wide variety of schools, whereas smaller-scale research that focuses on NLC is often held in contexts of higher AI/AN density and/or families with stronger cultural identification in which NLC can be expected to have more positive results. Thus, although they have previously shed a negative light on the use of NLC, the results from NAEP/NIES can provide a broader assessment that can contribute to a more nuanced understanding of how best to implement NLC in different contexts.

In planning for the implementation of NLC for AI/AN students with lower levels of cultural identification and/or in contexts of lower AI/AN student density, the literature on stereotype threat can provide useful guidance. For example, if students are encouraged to view intelligence as a malleable rather than fixed capacity, then they are less vulnerable to negative racial stereotypes regarding intelligence (Aronson, Fried, & Good, 2002; Good, Aronson, & Inzlicht, 2003). Blurring intergroup boundaries and reducing intergroup bias can also reduce the impact of stereotype threat (Rosenthal & Crisp, 2006). Similarly, reminding students of their membership in groups for which there are *positive* performance expectations (McGlone & Aronson, 2006) also reduces steretype threat. Research also suggests that simply teaching about stereotype threat before an assessment can reduce its negative effects (Johns, Schmader, & Martens, 2005). These findings suggest an expanded approach to NLC that includes these components may be more broadly effective with AI/AN students across a range of contexts.

Limitations and Conclusion

Several limitations should temper interpretation of these results. First, although NAEP/NIES is designed to be nationally representative, non-response among students, teachers, and administrators may create an unknown degree of bias in the results; additional replication of these results with other datasets is warranted. Second, the limitations of NIES surveys did not permit us to examine more nuanced aspects of NLC use in the classroom, such as how the teacher presented these concepts or how the students reacted. Further research is required to assess these details. Third, given the way in which teacher data were collected, we could not consider teachers as their own level in a nested/multilevel model. Thus, the results related to teachers may be biased to an unknown degree. Finally, since the data are cross-sectional (i.e., gathered at the same time), it is difficult to establish causality. It could be, for example, that causality is opposite of what was expected; specifically, schools with lower test scores could have been in the process of implementing NLC as a response mechanism, in which case the actual effects of NLC will be realized in future waves of data. Such hypotheses are not testable given the current structure of NAEP/NIES.

In spite of these limitations, our results add to the existing research by suggesting a more nuanced effect of NLC on student math achievement, which in turn calls for a more contextualized approach to the use of NLC in school settings. Rather than providing definitive answers on how to improve AI/AN students' academic achievement, our findings offer an important starting point for reconsidering how NLC can impact AI/AN students given their diversity in family backgrounds and learning environments.

Mark J. Van Ryzin *is a research scientist at the Oregon Research Institute (ORI) and serves on the faculty at the University of Oregon in the College of Education. His research focuses on social-ecological risk and protective processes related to parents, peers, teachers, and mentors; how these processes contribute to adolescent behavior and adjustment; and how school-based or community programs can be designed to intervene in these processes to prevent the escalation of problem behavior. His work is framed by a number of social/developmental theories, including attachment theory, self-determination theory, contact theory, and theories of coercion and social learning.*

Claudia G. Vincent *is a research associate in the Center for Equity Promotion (CEQP) at the University of Oregon. She focuses on promoting equitable school outcomes across students from various racial/ethnic backgrounds, abilities, and sexual orientations. Specific interests include school systems and teacher practices that promote positive teacher-student and peer relationships, improve students' perception of their classrooms as fair, and decrease the impact of biosocial stressors.*

NOTES

This research is supported by grant #R305A140162 (PI: J. Sprague) from the Institute of Educational Sciences (IES). The content is solely the responsibility of the authors and does not necessarily represent the official views of IES or the U.S. Department of Education. The authors recently analyzed reading achievement data from the same year (2011), as well as math achievement data from the previous NIES/NAEP dataset (2009), and found evidence corroborating the findings presented in this paper. Results of these analyses can be obtained from the first author.

1. These percentages were chosen to highlight the way different school contexts may impact AI/AN student math achievement, and therefore, they differ from the standard NIES definition of low density as less than 25% AI/AN students and high density as 25% or more AI/AN students.

REFERENCES

Apthorp, H. S., D'Amato, E. D., & Richardson, A. (2002). *Effective standards-based practices for Native American students: A review of research literature*. Washington, DC: U.S. Department of Education, Office of Educational Research and Improvement.

Aronson, J., Fried, C. B., & Good, C. (2002). Reducing the effects of stereotype threat on African American college students by shaping theories of intelligence. *Journal of Experimental Social Psychology, 38*(2), 113–125.

Aud, S., Hussar, W., Johnson, F., Kena, G., Roth, E., Manning, E., Wang, X., and Zhang, J. (2012). *The condition of education 2012*. (NCES 2012–045). Washington, DC: U.S. Department of Education, National Center for Education Statistics.

August, A., Goldenberg, C., & Rueda, R. (2006). Native American children and youth: Culture, language, and literacy. *Journal of American Indian Education, 45*(3), 24–37.

Beaulieu, D. (2006). A survey and assessment of culturally based education programs for Native American students in the United States. *Journal of American Indian Education, 45*(2), 50–61.

Bishop, R., Berryman, M., Cavanagh, T., & Teddy, L. (2009). Te kotahitanga: Addressing educational disparities facing Māori students in New Zealand. *Teaching and Teacher Education, 25*(5), 734–742.

Brayboy, B. M. J., & Castagno, A. E. (2009). Self-determination through self-education: Culturally responsive schooling for Indigenous students in the USA. *Teaching Education, 20*(1), 31–53.

Brayboy, B. M. J., Faircloth, S. C., Lee, T. S., Maaka, M. J., & Richardson, T. (2015). Indigenous education in the 21st century. Special issue. *Journal of American Indian Education, 54*(1).

Castagno, A. E., & Brayboy, B. M. J. (2008). Culturally responsive schooling for Indigenous youth: A review of the literature. *Review of Educational Research, 78*(4), 941–993.

Chavers, D. (2000). Indian teachers and school improvement. *Journal of American Indian Education, 39*(2), 1–18.

CHiXapkaid, Banks-Joseph, S. R., Inglebret, E., McCubbin, L. Sievers, J., Bruna, L., . . . & Sanyal, N. (2008). *From where the sun rises: Addressing the educational achievement of Native Americans in Washington State.* Pullman, WA: Washington State University, Clearinghouse on Native Teaching and Learning.

Demmert, W. G., Towner, J. C., & Yap, K. O. (2003). *A review of the research literature on the influences of culturally based education on the academic performance of Native American students.* Portland, OR: Northwest Regional Educational Laboratory.

Faircloth, S. C., & Tippeconnic III, J. W. (2010). *The dropout/graduation rate crisis among American Indian and Alaska Native Students: Failure to respond places the future of native peoples at risk.* Los Angeles, CA: The Civil Rights Project/Proyecto Derechos Civiles at UCLA.

Fryberg, S. A., Markus, H. R., Oyserman, D., & Stone, J. M. (2008). Of warrior chiefs and Indian princesses: The psychological consequences of American Indian mascots. *Basic and Applied Social Psychology, 30*(3), 208–218.

Good, C., Aronson, J., & Inzlicht, M. (2003). Improving adolescents' standardized test performance: An intervention to reduce the effects of stereotype threat. *Journal of Applied Developmental Psychology, 24*(6), 645–662.

Gutiérrez, K. D., & Rogoff, B. (2003). Cultural ways of learning: Individual traits or repertoires of practice. *Educational Researcher, 32*(5), 19–25.

Jesse, D., Meyer, S. J., & Klute, M. (2014). *Understanding factors related to American Indian and Alaska Native student achievement in reading and mathematics: Limited distribution report for the Native American Education Research Alliance.* Centennial, CO: Regional Educational Laboratory Central.

Johns, M., Schmader, T., & Martens, A. (2005). Knowing is half the battle: Teaching stereotype threat as a means of improving women's math performance. *Psychological Science, 16*(3), 175–179.

Keeshig-Tobias, L. (2003). Of hating, hurting, and coming to terms with the English language. *Canadian Journal of Native Education 27*(1), 89–100.

López, F. A., Heilig, J. V., & Schram, J. (2013). A story within a story: Culturally responsive schooling and American Indian and Alaska Native achievement in the National Indian Education Study. *American Journal of Education, 119*(4), 513–538.

Martinez, D. (2014). School culture and American Indian educational outcomes. *Procedia-Social and Behavioral Sciences, 116*, 199–205.

McCarty, T., & Lee, T. (2014). Critical culturally sustaining/revitalizing pedagogy and Indigenous education sovereignty. *Harvard Educational Review, 84*, 101–124.

McGlone, M. S., & Aronson, J. (2006). Stereotype threat, identity salience, and spatial reasoning. *Journal of Applied Developmental Psychology, 27*(5), 486–493.

National Center for Education Statistics (2013). *NAEP 2011 National Indian Education Study (NIES) restricted-use data files data companion* (NCES 2014476), by A.M. Rogers and J. J. Stoeckel. Washington, DC: U.S. Department of Education, Institute of Education Sciences.

National Education Association. (2010–2011). American Indians and Alaska Natives: Charting a new course for Native education. *Focus On American Indians and Alaska Natives* (pp. 2–3). Retrieved from NEA website: http://www.nea.org/assets/docs/AlAnfocus2010-2011.pdf

Powers, K. M. (2006). An exploratory study of cultural identity and culture-based educational programs for urban American Indian students. *Urban Education, 41*(1), 20–49.

Raudenbush, S. W., & Bryk, A. S. (2002). *Hierarchical linear models: Applications and data analysis methods* (Vol. 1). New York: Sage.

Richards, J. G., Vining, A. R., & Weimer, D. L. (2010). Aboriginal performance on standardized tests: Evidence and analysis from provincial schools in British Columbia. *Policy Studies Journal, 38*(1), 47–67.

Rosenthal, H. E., & Crisp, R. J. (2006). Reducing stereotype threat by blurring intergroup boundaries. *Personality and Social Psychology Bulletin, 32*(4), 501–511.

Smallwood, B. A., Haynes, E. F., & James, K. (2009). *English language acquisition and Navajo achievement in Magdalena, New Mexico: Promising outcomes in heritage language education*. Washington, DC: Center for Applied Linguistics.

Steele, C. M., & Aronson, J. (1995). Stereotype threat and the intellectual test performance of African Americans. *Journal of Personality and Social Psychology, 69*(5), 797–811.

Trujillo, O. V., & Alston, D. A. (2005). *A report on the status of American Indians and Alaska Natives in education: Historical legacy to cultural empowerment*. National Educational Association. Retrieved from http://www.nea.org/assets/docs/mf_aianreport.pdf

Tsethlikai, M. (2011). An exploratory analysis of American Indian children's cultural engagement, fluid cognitive skills, and standardized verbal IQ scores. *Developmental Psychology, 47*(1), 192–202.

Tsethlikai, M., & Rogoff, B. (2013). Involvement in traditional cultural practices and American Indian children's incidental recall of a folktale. *Developmental Psychology, 49*(3), 568–578.

Tyler, K. M., Uqdah, A. L., Dillihunt, M. L., Beatty-Hazelbaker, R., Conner, T., Gadson, N., . . . & Roan-Belle, C. (2008). Cultural discontinuity: Toward a quantitative investigation of a major hypothesis in education. *Educational Researcher, 37*(5), 280–297.

Van Ryzin, M. J., Vincent, C. G., & Hoover, J. (2016). Initial exploration of a construct representing Native language and culture (NLC) in elementary and middle school instruction. *Journal of American Indian Education, 55*(1), 74–101.

Authentically Authored Native American Young Adult Literature (YAL) and Culturally Sustaining Pedagogy (CSP) in the Preparation of Preservice Teachers

ALICE HAYS

College students in a young adult literature (YAL) course required for preservice teachers who are English education majors read the semi-autobiographical novel, *If I Ever Get Out of Here* (2013) by Eric Gansworth (Onandaga). Gansworth focuses on the experiences of a Tuscarora middle school student attending school off the reservation. At the conclusion of the course, students were surveyed to determine their perceptions of the social and political inequities explored in the novel. The survey sought to determine if reading this particular novel and participating in literature circles would prompt better understanding among non-Native students of the inequities inherent in the current social and educational system. The results indicated that the use of literature circles was *not* sufficient to develop a full understanding of the need for culturally sustaining pedagogy (CSP). Further work needs to be done in order to move beyond "scratching the surface" of white privilege and to generate realizations of inequity among preservice teachers.

"Cut if off," I yelled.

"Shut up, or my dad will hear you," Carson Mastick said. "He's not that drunk yet, and I'm gonna have a hard enough time explaining how you come down looking like a different kid than the one that went upstairs." For ten minutes, he'd been farting around, waving the scissors like a magic wand. Now he yanked the long tail of hair from my neck and touched the scissors an inch above my collar. "Is this about it? There's no turning back once I start chopping." (Gansworth, 2013, p. 3)

IN THIS SCENE FROM *If I Ever Get Out of Here* by Eric Gansworth (Onandaga), Tuscarora Reservation resident Lewis Black is about to take the unusual step of literally cutting off part of his heritage—his hair—which has been long all his life. Why would he do such a thing? As his friend's cousin astutely observes, it is so "the white kids will talk to [him]" (Gansworth, 2013, p. 3). Lewis is the only Indigenous (Native) student on the honors track in his predominantly white middle school, located just off the reservation. Although all of the students from his reservation attend this school when they enter sixth grade, he is the only reservation student in his level three honors class, making him the target of rampant bullying by the white students as well as the reservation students, albeit for different reasons. The white students bully him because of racism, and the Indian students bully him because of a sense of betrayal. Through Gansworth's fictionalized account, the reader vicariously experiences life on the reservation and its accompanying difficulties.

If I Ever Get Out of Here was a focus novel for ENG 471, Literature for Young Adults, an upper division course required for English education majors (it also fulfills upper division humanities credit for nonteaching students). I came to Arizona State University (ASU) as a white, female teacher with 19 years of English language arts (ELA) teaching experience in Arizona, where there are 21 federally recognized tribal nations. As a Ph.D. student interested in the ways that YAL generally shapes students' experiences, I sought an internship with Dr. James Blasingame, one of the foremost experts in the YAL field and a member of the ASU Red Ink Indigenous Initiative.[1] Dr. Blasingame took the lead on the course, and I taught several classes and co-facilitated our student-centered learning. ASU is a very large public state university situated only a few miles from the Salt River Pima-Maricopa Indian Community, the Fort McDowell Yavapai Nation, the Gila River Indian Community, Tohono O'odham Nation, and the Ak-Chin Indian Community. The University serves a highly diverse student population. Dr. Blasingame chose this novel after it was recommended to him by Debbie Reese (Nambé Pueblo), a leading expert on children's and young adult (YA) Indigenous literature. In 2014, *If I Ever Get Out of Here* was becoming one of the most decorated YA books on the market: garnering a 2014 Best Fiction for Young Adults award from the American Library Association's Young Adult Library Services Association, a 2014 Notable Books for a Global Society award from the International Reading Association, and award of the designation as a 2014 American Indian Youth Literary Awards Honor Book by the American Indian Library Association. Although we have a significant Native American population in Arizona, little, if any, of the curriculum in ASU's secondary ELA methods courses explores the nuanced depths of various Indigenous experiences. This lack of equity and deficit of exposure mandated a YA book by a Native author, written for and about Native youth. *If I Ever Get Out of Here*'s numerous recommendations for cultural authenticity and awards for excellence spurred the selection of Gansworth's novel.

If I Ever Get Out of Here is a raw depiction of life in the liminal space between the Tuscarora Reservation and the predominantly white community that surrounds the reservation. In the novel, Lewis, the protagonist, is entering a school outside the reservation where the majority of the students are white. Members of the surrounding community regard the Indigenous population as uncivilized. In fact, as young children, many of these students have been threatened with being sent to live with the "wild Indians" if they acted up (Gansworth, 2013, p.18). The school also serves youth from the military base, and Lewis meets George, whose family has just moved on base. George becomes Lewis's first friend from outside the reservation. Although Lewis visits George's home often, Lewis attempts to dissuade George from visiting his home on the reservation for fear George will realize the true depths of his poverty. Lewis continually doubts that George would want to be his true friend, although their love for the Beatles creates a deep bond between the two. Lewis also deals with significant bullying from Evan Reiniger, whose father gives a substantial amount of money to the school board, effectively protecting Evan from any potential punishments. While George and Lewis's friendship undergoes several trials, including micro-aggressions from George's girlfriend, George ultimately proves himself a true friend.

Lewis's skepticism about George's intentions and his distrust of the white community stem from a lifetime of inequities, abject poverty, and the racism that his Tuscarora family has experienced, including his mother's servitude to white families and his uncle's disillusionment with white society that resulted from his military service. As Uncle Albert tells Lewis about the two different communities or "planets" the two friends occupy, "we ain't got no rez rocket that's ever gonna get you to that other one, even though I know that's where you want to be" (Gansworth, 2013, p. 98). Albert goes on to tell Lewis that their planet is "just nice for *them*, not you" (p. 98). Armed with these warnings to not trust people from off the reservation, coupled with the prejudice he has experienced, Lewis has difficulty throughout the novel trusting George. For example, Lewis realizes that having a tarp as a kitchen wall is not the norm for people from communities like George's, and Lewis is unwilling to expose the depths of his poverty to someone he admires. Lewis's fears create a barrier between the two friends that they must overcome.

Because this novel addresses friendships between cultures in a powerful way, it ought to be regarded as a powerful, culturally sustaining teaching tool. The co-teacher and I chose to use Literature Circles (Daniels, 2006) as our pedagogy because the approach is student oriented and supports reader-response-based engagement (Rosenblatt, 1982) with in-depth issues. Literature circles are comprised of students who are divided into reading groups—either teacher-assigned or self-selected; each student within the group may be assigned various roles relative to the reading they might carry out (Daniels, 2006). Some of the typical roles used in literature circles include a discussion director, a literary luminary, an illustrator, and a vocabulary enricher. Our students rotated roles. While Daniels (2006) does not recommend keeping to strict roles for experienced and knowledgeable students, one of the objectives for our course was to provide students with pedagogical strategies they might take into their own ELA classrooms. Strictly following the original structure of the literature circles allowed our students to have a concrete understanding of the roles, which they could alter as necessary for their own students.

During the literature circles, I observed lively discussions that focused on many points of tension, including anger and disgust for bullying characters, curiosity about the cultural differences between the two primary characters, and for many, analysis of the quality of the relationships that occur within and outside reservation borders. While the literature circles were visibly successful in terms of active student engagement, I was curious to what degree students were vicariously experiencing the culture in the story and if students would be able to unpack their white privilege in order to deeply understand the inequities inherent in the society Gansworth describes. My interest motivated the research question: Would reading this novel prepare the preservice teachers in the class to appreciate CSP (Paris, 2012; Paris & Alim, 2014)?

If we, as educators, are attempting to create an educational system that "seeks to perpetuate and foster—*to sustain*—linguistic, literate, and cultural pluralism as part of the democratic project of schooling and as a needed response to demographic and social change" (Paris & Alim, 2014, p. 88), it is critical that we incorporate a variety of cultural voices within our classroom in a way that creates growth for all students. This need for CSP (Paris & Alim, 2014) is reiterated by the National Council of Teachers of English (NCTE) Position Statement in support of ethnic studies initiatives in K–12 curricula, approved and published in October of 2015, which suggests the need for teachers to:

> Provide students with texts that reflect their own cultural backgrounds and histories. In this way, educators can move beyond token multiculturalism to foster intercultural awareness and respect. These opportunities prove especially critical because implementation of the Common Core curriculum has led to a decline in representative diversity in classroom texts (NCTE, 2015).

How can we, as responsible educators at the secondary and postsecondary levels, expose our students to diverse cultures in a way that values and honors the reality of the cultures discussed without simultaneously "othering" those individuals who are of the culture under discussion? Providing students with the text is only a part of the equation; the other part must include a purposeful pedagogical approach. This study attempts to determine how effectively literature circles focused on authentically authored Native American YAL work to develop an appreciation for CSP.

Theoretical Framework

Evolution of Culturally Relevant Teaching

As power structures within society are continually renegotiated, so too are the conceptualization and application of culturally relevant pedagogy. Ladson-Billings's (1995) position on culturally relevant teaching (CRT) stems from the understanding that it must meet three criteria: "an ability to develop students academically, a willingness to nurture and support cultural competence, and the development of a sociopolitical or critical consciousness" (p. 483). The concept of CRT was further explored through Paris's (2012) development of the term culturally sustaining pedagogy (CSP), the idea that students' culture and linguistic practices must be valued in a long-term fashion, with the ultimate goal of developing a pluralistic education. McCarty and Lee (2014) expand on CSP by arguing that, for some cultures, the need for revitalization may be an additional concern, which brings us to culturally sustaining/revitalizing pedagogy (CSRP). These concepts, in various iterations, have been explored by multiple researchers and teacher educators: Castagno and Brayboy, 2008; Kirkness, 1999; Lafferty, 2014; Moll, Amanti,

Neff, and Gonzalez, 2009; Paris and Alim, 2014; White-Kaulaity, 2006; and Wyatt, 2009.

In *Culturally Responsive Teaching: Theory, Research and Practice*, Geneva Gay (2010) discusses a wide range of effective theoretical and pedagogical approaches to teaching in ways that value and honor nondominant cultures. Gay encourages the reader to understand why culturally responsive teaching is so critical and valuable for our young people; she simultaneously illustrates various approaches teachers might take to incorporate culturally responsive education within their own classrooms. For example, Gay states that culturally responsive teaching "uses the culture and experience of different ethnic groups as a launch pad for more effective teaching" (McClendon, 2012). A critical component of culturally responsive/sustaining/revitalizing teaching is the recognition that the literature used in an English course ought to contain the voices of the students within the classroom (Kirkness, 1999; Qureshi, 2006; White-Kaulaity, 2006).

One pedagogical approach that might address Gay's call for CRT includes literature circles, which "promote active and thoughtful stances toward reading" (Brabham & Villaume, 2000, p. 278). Importantly, literature circles enable students themselves to create the questions and discussion based on their prior experiences. This engagement can lead students to make meaningful connections with the text they are discussing (Brabham & Villaume, 2000; Daniels, 2006; McElvain, 2010). Student-text connections may help develop the classroom as a culturally responsive environment.

Critical Race Theory and TribalCrit

Indigenous voices are often the most marginalized voices in the classroom environment (Brayboy, 2005; Kirkness, 1999). In section 1.3.1, the Coolangatta statement explicates the present lack of equity in education:

> Invariably the nature, and consequently the outcome, of this education has been constructed through and measured by non-Indigenous standards, values and philosophies. Ultimately, the purpose of this education has been to assimilate Indigenous people into non-Indigenous cultures and societies. (Kirkness, 1999, p. 56)

The statement argues that "educational theories and practices have been developed and controlled by non-Indigenous people"; educational failure is a reality, but it is a failure of the system as opposed to a failure of Indigenous peoples (p. 56). The Coolangatta call to action asks us to recognize the importance of the teacher in the classroom as the facilitator of learning and to develop teacher preparation programs that support teachers in developing and implementing culturally inclusive curricula. The Coolangatta statement concludes, "Indigenous people have the right to be Indigenous [and] cannot exist as images and reflections of a non-Indigenous society" (p. 63).

Brayboy (2005) makes similar assertions while drawing upon the basis of Critical Race Theory: "Critical Race Theory [CRT] in education posits that racism is endemic in society and in education, and that racism has become so deeply engrained in society's and schooling's consciousness that it is often invisible" (p. 428). Brayboy argues that CRT must be developed in a way that addresses the liminal nature of American Indians' legal/political and racial experiences. Within his argument, he develops nine tenets of a tribally specific CRT that he terms TribalCrit. While all nine tenets are critical for the complete understanding of his theoretical framework, three are particularly relevant to this study, which explores how students recognize the liminal space of Indigenous peoples when reading authentically authored stories:

1. Indigenous peoples occupy a liminal space that accounts for both the political and racialized natures of our identities.
2. Concepts of culture, knowledge, and power take on new meaning when examined through an Indigenous lens.
3. Stories are not separate from theory; they make up theory and are therefore real and legitimate sources of data and ways of being (p. 429).

Using the theoretical frameworks of TribalCrit (Brayboy, 2005) and the Coolangatta statement (Kirkness, 1999), I explore how students' perspectives are influenced by reading an authentically authored novel, working from the hypothesis that demonstration of significant influence may indicate that preservice teachers within the course are moving toward a deeper appreciation of culturally sustaining pedagogy.

Literature Review

NCTE recognizes the need for student exposure to diverse literature and CSP in several position statements released on their website: the "Resolution on the Need for Diverse Children's and Young Adult

Books" (2015) and the "NCTE Position Statement in Support of Ethnic Studies Initiatives in K–12 Curricula" (2015). These statements and other research emphasize the need for all students to see themselves valued and honored within the mainstream curriculum (Castagno & Brayboy, 2008; Guillory, Wolverton, & Appleton, 2008; Kirkness, 1999; White-Kaulaity, 2006).

As White-Kaulaity (Diné) (2006) and Wyatt (2009) argue, the presence of Indigenous literature is imperative in our American classrooms, and non-Native teachers ought to incorporate this literature. Wyatt (2009) asserts that "[h]ow educators organize classrooms directly influences who has access to social and economic positions in greater society. This is accomplished by legitimizing certain forms of knowledge and regulating who has access to it" (p. 49). Wyatt also identifies increased academic success in CSP classrooms that contextualize learning within students' prior knowledge and experiences. Increased success, or cognitive support, is important for all students but particularly for Native students who "drop out of school at greater rates—and increasingly greater rates—than other population groups" (Reese, 2014, sec. 4).

White-Kaulaity (2006) hones this argument for Native American literature specifically. Her primary concern is that teachers "invite" voices into their classrooms. She exhorts us to self-reflect on our stated belief system. "If we truly value diversity within our culture, then we should teach this way. Too often, however, the Language Arts curriculum still excludes the Native American voice in favor of the 'voices of power,' the works of dominant culture" (p. 9). As Nambé Pueblo scholar Reese (2014) suggests, Native American students' self-esteem and self-efficacy may be positively impacted through the inclusion of authentically authored literature throughout their education, while non-Natives will also benefit from the inclusion of accurate stories. This rallying cry is also taken up by Bista (2012), who pushes for classroom inclusion of authentic authors of young adult and children's literature. The goal of Native-authored literature is to "not just . . . understand, accept, and appreciate cultural differences, but also to ultimately transform the existing social order in order to ensure greater voice and authority to the marginalized cultures and to achieve social equality and justice among all" (p. 317).

Much research on preservice teachers and their culturally sustaining pedagogical preparation speaks of guiding predominantly white, female teachers toward awareness of and knowledge about the diversity within their classrooms (Goodwin et al., 2014; Gordon, 2005; Martin &

Van Gunten, 2002; Paris, 2012; Sleeter, 2001). For example, McFalls and Cobb-Roberts (2001) discuss a study in which preservice teachers are introduced to the concept of cognitive dissonance in order to decrease resistance to ideas that do not fit within their preconceived version of reality. Festinger (1957) hypothesized that "the existence of dissonance, being psychologically uncomfortable, will motivate the person to try to reduce the dissonance and achieve consonance" (p. 3). Little research, however, focuses on how we might educate teachers by moving them toward productive discomfort (rather than cognitive dissonance). I define *productive discomfort* as the moment when students are confronted with a reality at odds with their prior experience and are able to grapple with new understandings that may bring about intellectual or emotional growth as opposed to rejecting that reality to maintain their inner sense of equilibrium. In order to address the diverse needs within multicultural classrooms, especially to address Native American needs, this productive discomfort must occur for educators. While some evidence indicates that community involvement and action research may affect preservice teacher attitudes (Sleeter, 2001), the use of literature circles to help move Indigenous theory into practice has not been explored in this way.

Methodology

Participant Characteristics

The study participants were enrolled in an upper-level undergraduate course titled, Literature for Today's Young Adults. The course is open to anyone and is a requirement for preservice teachers. The class typically consists of 50% preservice teachers, 40% literature students, and 10% other, although the researcher did not collect this information about the students who participated in this study.

All students were given the option to take the survey. Thirty-five of the 54 students opted to complete the survey. Of the students who responded, 28 identified as female, seven identified as male, and two identified as "other." There were 13 students between the ages of 18–20; 21 students between the ages of 21–29; two students between the ages of 30–39; and one student between the ages of 40–49. The respondents were given the option to self-identify by racial or ethnic categories. The results of the self-identification included: two American Indian or Alaskan Native students, three Latino/a students, two Asian/Pacific Islander students, one black/African American student, one Khazarian Jewish student, and four multi-ethnic students who filled in "other" with the following labels: Asian/Pacific Islander and Caucasian, black/Mexican, white/Asian, and Native American/Caucasian. Twenty-one students self-identified as white/Caucasian. In data analysis, I included the multi-ethnic Native American/Caucasian student in the Native American category as her/his survey responses seemed to demonstrate prior experience within an active Native American culture. The terms Native American, Indigenous, and American Indian are contested; when possible I use tribal affiliation for each individual and Indigenous when referring to a group. The survey gave students the option to self-identify as Native American.

Pedagogy

When we began reading *If I Ever Get Out of Here*, we asked students to self-select into groups of five to six members. We supplied the students with a packet containing descriptions of various literature-circle roles as discussed previously, and asked the students to select one role per class period. The plan was for each student to experience each role at least once throughout the process. During the next several weeks, the groups would gather and discuss the novel following the roles they had chosen. The groups were completely self-directed, and the instructors traveled around the room listening in on their discussions. This study was limited in that the researcher did not record or memo observations from the literature circles, so the findings are based exclusively on the survey that was administered at the end of the semester, two months after finishing the novel. The survey was given as a supplemental handout with their final exam, and students were given the option to anonymously participate.

Survey Instrument and Data Analysis

Participants were asked to complete two open-ended survey questions: (1) What did you notice about the relationship between the Native community and the non-Native community as portrayed by Eric Gansworth? (2) Upon reflection, what conclusions about the Native community and non-Native community did you come to? On average, each participant wrote two to five sentences per response, although three outliers wrote close to half a page per question. The responses were diverse and resulted in 23 different categories identified through initial coding processes as discussed in the following paragraph.

I retyped all survey results into separate documents and uploaded each document into the coding software, NVivo. I divided the data into multiple internal folders identified by questions and racial self-identifications. For example, one set of folders was titled Indigenous Q1, which consisted of all documents that contained responses to question one from my self-identified Native American participants, and another set was labeled Indigenous Q2, which consisted of all documents that contained responses to question two from the same participants. I continued this labeling process for each self-identified ethnicity and their question one and two responses.

NVivo has the ability to run a word query, which identifies the frequency of repeated words within the documents. The most repeated words were a direct result of the word choices in the initial question (Native American, community, and relationship) so I removed these words from my initial search within the folders for repeated words. Words that were identified as highly occurring included "misunderstandings" and "differences." I began with a holistic coding approach (Saldaña, 2013) to search for evidence of misunderstandings and differences. I quickly realized that these particular terms did not fully encompass the in-depth themes that were emerging. I then turned to a constant comparative method (Glaser, 1965) to identify the themes and nodes that were the most prevalent. Glaser suggests the researcher must maintain a flexible sense of the data and consistently return to the information to generate and suggest general categories and hypotheses about the problems under study. For example, I included multiple ideas under one node titled "differences," including differences due to culture, fear, hate, racism or prejudice, integration or assimilation, unfairness, and misunderstandings. Upon revisiting the specific comments, a constant theme emerged: "the contribution to interracial tensions," which I may have missed had I not been flexible. I also used discourse analysis (Gee, 2014a, 2014b) within the theoretical framework of CSRP and TribalCrit to identify words or ideas that supported or challenged the culturally and linguistically responsive goals of teaching this novel. For example, the use of the phrase "wrongly prejudiced against" indicates some understanding of the inequities experienced by Indigenous peoples, thereby touching upon the politicized nature of the liminal space occupied by Indigenous peoples.

Findings

Five themes emerged relative to the question of how this novel influenced student perspectives: the novel's authenticity, an equal contribution to interracial tensions, historical factors, inequities, and realized understandings. The Indigenous students in the classroom found the novel to be important in several ways, while non-Native students were less inclined to see the significance of the novel beyond their own experience.

Authenticity of the Novel

Holistic coding revealed an important theme of judging the novel *If I Ever Get Out of Here* as realistic or accurate. Two of the Indigenous participants felt the novel was a realistic portrayal of the community; they stated that Gansworth provided "truth in history" and discussed "real issues." One Indigenous respondent wrote that s/he "liked Gansworth's decision to provide readers with a different perspective from an American Indian teenager." This comment points to a significant implication: that the American Indian experience is not currently included within our educational system and may be sorely missed.

An Indigenous/Caucasian participant wrote, "Gansworth hits on real issues that real people had to deal with and he does this very well." It is interesting to note that s/he uses "real" to modify both issues and people. While the novel is semi-autobiographical fiction, the respondent's self-identification with the situations demonstrates a powerful component of how YAL can mirror back to students who they are (Qureshi, 2006). Another strength of YAL can be its function as a window through which students may more accurately see others (Bishop, 1990; Galda & Cox, 1990).

While the Indigenous participants identified the novel as realistic, only one participant out of the 33 non-Native respondents mentioned the novel's authenticity in any way. This white respondent wrote, "I think how the people are portrayed was fairly accurate. Yes, it was told through a young child, so I am sure it is different, but the base points seemed to be true." If our goals of encouraging CSRP are to be realized, it is important that readers see the issues as realistic and relevant to the world outside the pages of this novel. If non-Native students who may become teachers do not recognize the novel's authenticity, there is a danger that Indigenous people will continue to be relegated to the liminal space of the politicized classroom, as discussed by Brayboy (2005).

Equal Contribution to Tension

Despite Gansworth's (2013) blatant portrayal of the imbalanced living and educational situations that negatively impacted the Native community, a surprising theme emerged: the Native and non-Native communities were equally to blame for tensions between the two. While half of the white respondents wrote some version of the claim that "both sides were guilty of racism," only one-third of the other respondents made a similar claim. We can see an interesting disparity in the language that the respondents used to define the source of tension. Using discourse analysis (Gee, 2014a, 2014b), I tracked the use of words with negative connotations, such as "hostility" and "judgment." One white respondent stated that "[t]here was a lot of hostility and resentment on both sides, and a desire to keep the cultures separate from each other." Based upon the actions Lewis took in the beginning of the novel, however, he did not evince a desire to keep the cultures separate. Another white participant wrote that the "disdain and hate between the native and non-native community is obvious." On the other hand, the Indigenous participants used words such as "misunderstanding," which is discussed later when identifying the cause of the tension between the communities. The difference in word choice between the Indigenous participants and the non-Native participants is notable. The closest any of the Indigenous students came to using words such as "hostile" or "hate" to describe the relations between communities in the novel came from the response of a multi-ethnic Indigenous/Caucasian student who wrote, "The portrayal of almost disgust between the non-native community toward the native community is written very well."

Another important distinction between Native and non-Native respondents is the use of "between" versus "toward." The white student used "between," which implies that there is some level of equity between the two groups, while the Indigenous/white student wrote as though the Native community was on the receiving end of negativity. This disparity reinforces the idea that the concepts of power shift when viewed through an Indigenous lens (Brayboy, 2005).

When considering whether reading an authentically authored piece coupled with literature circles would support preservice teachers in becoming practitioners of CSRP, I find it problematic that some of the white students, who represent the majority of our teaching force, apply equal blame for the tension within the novel. One interesting response by a white student exemplifies this trend: "A lot of resistance from both sides. Neither justified." I suspect that this participant might have responded differently if s/he had identified more viscerally with the protagonist. Lewis is physically attacked several times a day for several weeks at school, and when he attempts to talk to administration about it, he is dismissed immediately. Lewis is justified in his resistance to the dominant culture. Another respondent (white) wrote that the "main character had strong feelings towards non-natives which were perpetuated by the bullying he received." Given that Lewis cut off his hair in order to fit in with the culture at his school, this comment seems to be a case of putting the result before the cause. If this lack of awareness among preservice teachers causes them to misinterpret their students' resistance from the margins, there may be problems within the classroom.

I have discussed the white respondents and the way they viewed both communities as problematic. The data analysis shows that one-half of the participants who identified as multi-ethnic used words similar to the white respondents. They wrote, for example, "[t]here seemed to be a bit of hostility on each side towards the other," and "both communities pass unfair judgment because of the vast differences." This similarity may be attributed to their personal identification at the time of the survey. This finding reinforces the importance of incorporating a wide variety of voices within the English classroom in order to achieve CSRP (McCarty & Lee, 2014). I had wondered if traditionally marginalized groups would demonstrate a stronger acknowledgment of inequities presented in the novel. The findings indicate, however, that these students did not identify with Lewis any more significantly than the white students did, further emphasizing the need to incorporate a wide variety of nondominant literature in our English courses, with specific emphasis on rarely included Indigenous literature.

Historical Factors

Six respondents mentioned "history" or "the past," and the way that participants spoke about history was important to consider in light of how they might view modern relationships between Native and non-Native communities. One student (Khazarian Jewish) wrote:

> History matters. The conquest of North America long a fait accompli, the whites assume the natives judge success by the same metrics. To assume that another people desire to live the way of their conquerors is

the height of presumptuousness. We should allow people their own standards, not force or project ours onto them.

The preceding quote may reference the idea that Lewis's home did not meet the white community's norms, and Lewis recognized this fact. He assumed that George would judge him according to those white norms, which have been passed down through settler-colonial society. One wonders if there were a greater balance of stories that addressed the contemporary realities of nondominant cultures, would the sense of shame discussed in this semi-autobiographical book continue to be expressed? As Reese (2014) discusses, "Native students do not see themselves reflected in the curriculum." I would add that the limited literature that is part of the curriculum is not representative of the contemporary Indigenous peoples' story as theory (Brayboy, 2005) but instead represents history through the dominant culture's lens.

Not all respondents, for example, identify Lewis's current living situation as one of inequity, but they do recognize the negative impact of the American Holocaust. A white participant wrote, "I feel that the novel helped me to understand how the treatment of native communities in the past affects generations today. I've concluded that the treatment of the past still affects communities greatly for generations afterwards." Although students recognize that colonialism has negatively influenced relationships among Indigenous peoples and whites, they do not necessarily recognize that colonial processes and a grave imbalance of power are ongoing, or that students are inadvertently complicit.

Some of the reactions to cultural disparities may be related to defensiveness on the part of the participants. One white respondent wrote: "It made me realize that there are probably plenty of Native Americans who are able to forgive and not hold on to the mistakes of past generations (not hold on to the bitterness)." The discourse here identifies the problem as people who cannot forgive others for wrongdoing. The identification of past generations lays culpability on someone other than the student and his/her generation. Identifying Indigenous peoples as being "able" to forgive others for "mistakes" positions the Indigenous peoples as possibly being incapable of forgiveness, or weakened in some way, while simultaneously positioning the perpetrators of violence towards Indigenous peoples as "accidentally" genocidal. One might assume that this participant would not actively participate in the brutal actions committed by white settlers, however the defensive belief that it is "all in the past" may be harmful to future students and does not encourage our society to address current wrongs. Applying the

Indigenous lens discussed in Brayboy (2005) may move these preservice teachers toward the productive discomfort necessary for growth, as opposed to this self-absolvent thinking.

Inequities

While ten students felt that the novel's intercommunity tensions were due to a lack of communication, nine students identified inequity as a basic cause. All the Indigenous participants mentioned some version of inequity or unfairness in their responses. For example, one Indigenous participant wrote: "I notice the vast difference between the native community and non-native community, even though they are in the same country. One is poor, and under-privilege, while the other is doing okay and privilege. There is unfairness between them, socially and personally." Another Indigenous participant wrote, "The native community is also treated [more] unfairly than the non-native community." A third Indigenous participant related a story about how difficult her great grandmother's life was due to "differences between on res and off res life"; so much so that she ran away to live on a different reservation. This respondent identified current prejudices that are "hindering progression." These responses assert a continuity between the inequities in the novel and in the respondents' lived experiences. They see inequity as real, a significant contributing factor to the tensions between Native and non-Native communities. As Brayboy (2005) posits, the imbalance of power within the novel was, in fact, visible to the class participants who engaged in the reading through an Indigenous lens.

While two of the responses from the white students mentioned some sort of inequity, the language surrounding their responses was less specific about who suffers from the inequities, which may indicate an attempt to absolve themselves of culpability as white members of society. For example, one respondent writes, "Gansworth clearly separates the two communities through their lifestyles, lingos, cultural traditions and socioeconomic circumstances." This statement briefly nods at the disparities in financial situations but couches this disparity among other characteristics (cultural traditions, for example) that might be "celebrated" differences rather than unfair inequities. Several respondents were clearly cognizant of the inequity portrayed throughout the novel: "The tension from the natives was reasonable because of the cruelty they experienced from the non-native community"; "There's a significant divide between the native community and the non-native community both because of racial differences and the disparity between middle-class and poverty"; and "we have a long way to go in the fair treatment of native people." These observations seem hopefully reflective of an influence on students and future educators to respect and use a CSP approach, but those who absolve themselves of culpability avoid the productive discomfort necessary for growth.

Unexpected Realizations

Eight of the participants had apparently never been made aware of the differences between Native and non-Native living conditions and experiences. For example, one white respondent wrote, "Coming from the background I have, it's crazy to think of being treated the same way the Indian community was." Another respondent stated, "I thought that the native community has so much to overcome that *I never realized* [emphasis added]." Critical realizations such as these are necessary for preservice teachers to open up conversations, to create change, and to consider how they wield and share power within their classrooms.

Discussion

Proponents of culturally responsive teaching and CSP in the English language arts classroom point to the need to move away from the current monolingual society, where only the voice of white culture is valued through curricular choices and teaching activities (Castagno & Brayboy, 2008; Gay, 2010; Paris, 2012; Paris & Alim, 2014; White-Kaulaity, 2006). Whereas ENG 471: Young Adult Literature is not specifically a multicultural course, the specific focus on novels and teaching techniques that preservice teachers might use in their own classrooms lends itself well to the propagation of CSP. As A. Nilsen, Blasingame, Donelson, and Nilsen, (2013) argue, multicultural YAL can be important to all students as "[y]oung readers can identify with characters who straddle two worlds because they have similar experiences in going between the worlds of adulthood and childhood" (p. 97). Traversing cultural boundaries may be particularly true for many Indigenous students, who are often forced into liminal spaces by attending secondary schools off the reservation. While YAL may positively reflect Indigenous students and support their emergence from those liminal spaces into the mainstream classroom, culturally appropriate YAL may be just as beneficial for other students. For example, students who are members of the dominant culture may be able to see significant differences among the individual members of the nondominant culture, which can lend itself to a deeper understanding of the people around all of us (Nilsen et al., 2013).

The inclusion of an Indigenously authored novel, combined with a student-driven pedagogy, seemed to be an obvious way to incorporate CSRP within our course (McCarty & Lee, 2014). Our findings indicate a level of success with students who self-identified as Indigenous. Survey responses indicate that the course touched upon the criteria necessary to achieve Ladson-Billings's (1995) calls to culturally relevant teaching (CRT), including an ability to develop students academically and a willingness to nurture and support cultural competence. The third criteria for Ladson-Billings's CRT, however, is that students develop a "sociopolitical and critical consciousness" (p. 483). While one-third of the white students seemed to demonstrate a newfound awareness of sociopolitical and critical consciousness through their survey responses, the students' reactions do not strongly indicate that we created future educators who have a "willingness to nurture and support cultural competence" (Ladson-Billings, 1995, p. 483). While the students reacted positively to the novel as a whole, and the surveys indicate increasing awareness of cultural experiences, I cannot say with confidence that the preservice teachers saw enough importance in this story to include this novel and others like it within their classrooms.

Paris's (2012) call to teach in a pluralistic fashion by exposing all students to all cultures, thereby helping them to recognize and value each one of these various iterations of human experience, was not fully realized. The students were not asked to vividly explore their notions of Indigenous culture in a significant way. Their lack of in-depth understanding was evidenced through their survey responses. While some students did appear to gain a different understanding of a culture other than their own, not all students demonstrated this level of comprehension. The shortcomings of what we accomplished cannot be wholly or solely attributed to the students, however.

CSRP emphasizes the importance of student voice, and literature circles provide that opportunity for students. Provided a teacher has a diverse classroom environment, s/he might believe that students would walk away from a novel study with a broader understanding of the text and, in this particular case, a more intimate understanding of one person's experience on the Tuscarora reservation. However, literature circles may not be enough to help all students understand the more nuanced, or even obvious, components of a text if they do not bring prior knowledge or experience about an issue to the conversation. While we used literature circles and the observed engagement of the students seemed to be fairly strong, we realized that some of the more significant areas of multiculturalism did not "stick with" the students, at least after two months had passed.

One of our goals, through the use of YAL, was to help future educators recognize that choices of content, such as novels, organize their classrooms in ways that reflect and influence sociopolitical environments. We initially believed that using a student-centered pedagogical model to introduce students to novels that met the criteria of CSP scholars would result in students' thoughtful reflection and increased cultural awareness. Survey results indicate our hopes were only partly realized. Some white students became aware of their lack of knowledge: "It was very eye-opening to the way Native Americans lived. I never would have understood this without reading the novel." It is possible however, that all we did was scratch the surface of white privilege. As McIntosh (1990) discusses in "Unpacking the Knapsack of White Privilege," many whites are taught to see racism as something that puts others at a disadvantage, yet they are not taught the corollary of white privilege; consequently, it is very difficult for many white people to acknowledge race as an issue. Understanding the role whites play in perpetuating systemic racism generates discomfort for many in the dominant white culture, which may be a component of the stubborn resistance to address the issue of race head-on (Castagno & Brayboy, 2008; Wyatt, 2009). Providing our students with a stronger, more focused lens, such as CSRP, to discuss the material may lead these students to the educational goals we have set for them.

Implications

As teacher educators, we are responsible for preparing preservice teachers to be aware of diversity and to teach in culturally respectful and culturally sustaining ways. In order to prepare teachers for the important work of CSRP, teacher educators must actively consider the ways they address multicultural education and pedagogical approaches. Will a quality YA novel from an Indigenous author combined with a respected pedagogical tool accomplish these goals? While these tools certainly open the door for this potentiality, the students' surveys show gaps in their understanding of the causes of tension or ongoing systemic inequities. The novel and literature circles alone are not enough to generate productive discomfort—the moment when participants recognize the power of the dominant culture and the ways in which this power contributes to social inequities.

We started with the assumption that using a good book with an authentic voice would achieve our goals, but the results we achieved are mixed. How might we lead future teachers to the necessary productive discomfort and consequent cognitive dissonance necessary for deep change? We could assign readings that prime them to think about the novel through an Indigenous lens, such as the Coolangatta statement (Kirkness, 1999) and Brayboy's article on TribalCrit Theory. Providing these lenses to students prior to reading the novel, and then having them participate in literature circles, might have the desired impact. It also might be effective to incorporate this theoretical framework after reading the novel and then returning to the discussion involving the book. We must continue to work to help our preservice teachers see Native and non-Native inequities as important and recognize their own inadvertent complicity in order to create true change. As one Indigenous participant stated: "What I learned about the non-native community is that they are clueless about Native life, which is why this book needs to be taught and read. There are not many Native books being taught or read. These stories need to be mainstream in order to understand Native Americans."

We must rethink not only the types of literature being taught, thereby shifting the perception of what a seminal American text might be, but we must also rethink the instructional approaches used to support students as they become civic-minded members of our society. The theoretical frameworks of CSP and Brayboy's Tribal Critical Race Theory (2005) speak well to this shift. Productive discomfort is necessary to enact systemic change; cognitive dissonance may be created through effective and engaging curriculum. As teacher educators, we must help our future educators recognize the voices of those who do not have power in the mainstream classroom. Honoring these silenced voices in the classroom can be the important first step in true social change.

Alice Hays *is an Assistant Professor of Education at California State, Bakersfield. Her research focuses on the pedagogical implications of young adult literature within the secondary classroom, and the ways in which teachers approach this instruction. She has 19 years of secondary teaching experience.*

NOTES

1. The Red Ink Initiative is an interrelated set of campus, regional, national, and international projects, including an international journal, to achieve its

mission and goals in collaboration with Indigenous communities. For more information, see https://english.clas.asu.edu/research/community-university-initiatives/red-ink-indigenous-initiative.

REFERENCES

Bishop, R. S. (1990). Windows and mirrors: Children's books and parallel cultures. *Illinois English Bulletin, 78*(1), 83.

Bista, K. (2012). Multicultural literature for children and young adults. *The Educational Forum, 76*(3), 317–325.

Brabham, E. G., & Villaume, S. K. (2000). Continuing conversations about literature circles. *Reading Teacher, 54*(3), 278–280. Retrieved from http://content.ebscohost.com.ezproxy.webfeat.lib.ed.ac.uk/ContentServer.asp?T=P&P=AN&K=3743371&S=R&D=afh&EbscoContent=dGJyMMTo5oSeqLM4y9f3OLCmroqeprVSsqu4SreWxWXS&ContentCustomer=dGJyMPGprkmxprVMuePfgeyx43zx\nhttp://ezproxy.lib.ed.ac.uk/login?url=http://

Brayboy, B. M. J. (2005). Toward a Tribal Critical Race Theory in education. *The Urban Review, 37*(5), 425–446. doi:10.1007/s11256-005-0018-y

Castagno, A. E., & Brayboy, B. M. J. (2008). Culturally responsive schooling for Indigenous youth: A review of the literature. *Review of Educational Research, 78*(4), 941–993. doi:10.3102/0034654308323036

Daniels, H. (2006). What's the next big thing with literature circles? *Voices from the Middle, 13*(4), 10–15.

Festinger, L. (1957). *A theory of cognitive dissonance.* Stanford, CA: Stanford University Press.

Galda, L., & Cox, S. (1990). Children's books: Multicultural literature: Mirrors and windows on a global community. *The Reading Teacher, 43*(8), 582–589. Retrieved from http://www.jstor.org.ezproxy1.lib.asu.edu/stable/20200477

Gansworth, E. (2013). *If I ever get out of here.* New York: Arthur A. Levine Books.

Gay, G. (2010). *Culturally responsive teaching* (2nd ed.). New York and London: Teacher's College Press.

Gee, J. P. (2014a). *An introduction to discourse analysis: Theory and method* (4th ed.). London, England: Routledge.

Gee, J. P. (2014b). *How to do discourse analysis: A toolkit.* London, England: Routledge.

Glaser, B. G. (1965). The constant comparative method of qualitative analysis. *Social Problems, 12*(4), 436–445. Retrieved from http://www.jstor.org/stable/798843

Goodwin, A. L., Smith, L., Souto-Manning, M., Cheruvu, R., Tan, M. Y., Reed, R., & Taveras, L. (2014). What should teacher educators know and be able to do? Perspectives from practicing teacher educators. *Journal of Teacher Education*, (May), 1–19. doi:10.1177/0022487114535266

Gordon, J. (2005). Inadvertent complicity: Colorblindness in teacher education. *Educational Studies, 38*(2), 135–153.

Guillory, R., Wolverton, M., & Appleton, V. (2008). American Indian/Alaska Native voices in the model of institutional adaptation to student diversity. *Journal of American Indian Education, 47*(2), 51–75.

Kirkness, V. J. (1999). The Coolangatta statement on indigenous rights in education. *Journal of American Indian Education, 39*(1), 1–20.

Ladson-Billings, G. (1995). Toward a theory of culturally relevant pedagogy. *American Educational Research Journal, 32*(3), 465–491.

Lafferty, K. E. (2014). "What are you reading?" How school libraries can promote racial diversity in multicultural literature. *Multicultural Perspectives, 16*(4), 203–209. doi:10.1080/15210960.2014.951888

Martin, R. J., & Van Gunten, D. M. (2002). Reflected identities applying positionality and multicultural social reconstructionism in teacher education. *Journal of Teacher Education, 53*(1), 44–54.

McCarty, T. L., & Lee, T. (2014). Critical culturally sustaining/revitalizing pedagogy and Indigenous education sovereignty. *Harvard Educational Review, 84*(1), 101–124.

McClendon, G. (2012). Geneva Gay. YouTube. Retrieved from https://www.youtube.com/watch?v=3gnI4bn9bUY

McElvain, C. M. (2010). Transactional literature circles and the reading comprehension of English learners in the mainstream classroom. *Journal of Research in Reading, 33*(2), 178–205. doi:10.1111/j.1467-9817.2009.01403

McFalls, E. L., & Cobb-Roberts, D. (2001). Reducing resistance to diversity through cognitive dissonance instruction: Implications for teacher education. *Journal of Teacher Education, 52*(2), 164–172. Retrieved from http://doi.org/10.1177/0022487101052002007

McIntosh, P. (1990). Unpacking the knapsack of white privilege. *Independent School, 49*(2), 31–36. Retrieved from http://insightpv.org/storage/Microsoft Word - Unpacking the Knapsack of White Privilege.pdf

Moll, L. C., Amanti, C., Neff, D., & Gonzalez, N. (2009). Funds of knowledge for teaching: Using a qualitative approach to connect homes and classrooms. *Theory Into Practice, 31*(2), 132–141. doi:10.1080/00405849209543534

NCTE Position statement in support of ethnic studies initiatives in K–12 curricula. (2015). Retrieved January 12, 2017, from http://www.ncte.org/positions/statements/ethnic-studies-k12-curr

NCTE Resolution on the need for diverse children's and young adult books. (2015). Retrieved January 12, 2017, from http://www.ncte.org/positions/statements/diverse-books

Nilsen, A., Blasingame, J., Donelson, K., & Nilsen, D. (2013). *Literature for today's young adults* (9th ed.). Boston: Pearson.

Paris, D. (2012). Culturally sustaining pedagogy: A needed change in stance, terminology, and practice. *Educational Researcher, 41*(3), 93–97.

Paris, D., & Alim, H. S. (2014). What are we seeking to sustain through culturally sustaining pedagogy? A loving critique forward. *Harvard Educational Review, 84*(1), 85–100. doi:10.17763/haer.84.1.982l873k2ht16m77

Qureshi, K. S. (2006). Beyond mirrored worlds: Teaching world literature to challenge students' perceptions of others. *The English Journal, 96*(2), 34–40. Retrieved from http://www.jstor.org/stable/30047125

Reese, D. (2014). Why AICL matters. Retrieved January 3, 2017 from https://americanindiansinchildrensliterature.blogspot.com/p/about.html

Rosenblatt, L. M. (1982). The literary transaction: Evocation and response. *Theory Into Practice, 21*(March 2015), 268–277. http://doi.org/10.1080/00405848209543018

Saldaña, J. (2013). *The coding manual for qualitative researchers* (2nd ed.). Los Angeles, London, New Delhi, Singapore, Washington DC: SAGE Publications.

Sleeter, C. E. (2001). Preparing teachers for culturally diverse schools: Research and the overwhelming presence of whiteness. *Journal of Teacher Education, 52*(2), 94–106. doi:10.1177/0022487101052002002

White-Kaulaity, M. (2006). The voices of power and the power of voices: *The ALAN Review, 34*(1), 8–16.

Wyatt, T. (2009). The role of culture in culturally compatible education. *Journal of American Indian Education, 48*(3), 47–63.

Learning Through Language: Academic Success in an Indigenous Language Immersion Kindergarten

LINDSAY A. MORCOM AND STEPHANIE ROY

What are the academic results of Anishinaabemowin (Ojibwe language) immersion education at the Mnidoo Mnising Anishinaabek Kinoomaage Gamig (MMAK) early learning kindergarten program? We describe the development of the MMAK within the context of larger language and education policies in the community and Canada. We also examine the academic development of junior and senior kindergarten students in the program. Using the Early Years Evaluation Teacher Assessment (EYE-TA), we assess participants' holistic development, including their cognitive development and English language acquisition. Although students show some delay in the first months of immersion education, by the end of the second year the average student shows age-appropriate cognitive and linguistic development. This promising outcome indicates that Indigenous language immersion does not negatively impact educational achievement or mainstream language acquisition; on the contrary, it likely provides benefits to students in these and other areas.

FIRST NATIONS CHILDREN IN CANADA today inherit a complex educational legacy. On one hand, they inherit as a birthright access to Indigenous intellectual and educational traditions that span millennia. On the other hand, they inherit a legacy of colonial education that sought to destroy Indigenous cultures and languages, with devastating consequences (Truth and Reconciliation Commission [TRC], 2015b). Due to this legacy, the vast majority of Indigenous languages in Canada are now endangered (Campbell, 1997; UNESCO, 2014), and the high school completion rate of First Nations people living on-reserve is less than 41% (Statistics Canada, 2011; in TRC, 2015b). This rate is significantly lower than the high school completion rate of First Nations people living off-reserve (60%) and less than half of the national Canadian average (88%) (Statistics Canada, 2011; in TRC, 2015b).

Currently, First Nations are moving toward increased Indigenous culturally sustaining and immersion education (Assembly of First Nations, 2010). The move comes at an important time, when the completion of the TRC has resulted in new calls to action for reconciliation in Canada (TRC, 2015a). Now more than ever, community-based practitioners and scholars of Indigenous education are confronting the dominant colonial system of education. They are rethinking education from a critical standpoint that integrates resistance, renewal, and reclamation and that embraces a culturally sustaining pedagogy (CSP) (Paris & Alim, 2014). CSP seeks to preserve and maintain the diverse multitude of languages, literacies, and cultures in our global society. Taking a firm position of sustaining pluralism in education is necessary. Advocacy for pluralism allows Indigenous immersion programs like the one described here to reframe education in ways that embrace Indigenous ways of knowing and being. For far too long an assimilationist monolingual and monocultural education has been defined as the standard approach in First Nations across Canada and the United States (TRC, 2015b). Indigenous education systems in North America are increasingly resisting this monolinguistic standard (Hermes, Bang, & Marin, 2012). Instituting Indigenous language immersion (ILI) is an act of reclamation, strength, identity, and inherent sovereignty (AFN, 2010; Battiste, 2013; Morcom, 2013, 2014; TRC, 2015b; UNESCO, 2014; Usborne, Peck, Smith, & Taylor, 2011).

Numerous communities across North America have developed ILI programs for their languages. Of note, the communities of the Mi'kmaq Kina'matnewey in Nova Scotia have seen their language move from endangered to vulnerable status according to UNESCO's evaluation criteria; they have also achieved a high school graduation rate of 87.7% through CSP and ILI education (Battiste, 2013; TRC, 2015b; UNESCO, 2014; Usborne et al., 2011). ILI programs have also been developed for Inuttitut (Bougie, Wright, & Taylor, 2003; Louis & Taylor, 2001; Wright & Taylor, 1995), Hualapai (Watahomigie & McCarty, 1994), Blackfoot (Kipp, 2000), Arapaho (Greymorning, 1995), Mohawk (Agbo, 2001; White, 2015), Navajo (Lockard & de Groat, 2010), and Maliseet (Perley, 2011), among others (Ball, 2007; DeJong, 1998; Demmert, 2001; Grenoble & Whaley, 2006; Guèvremont & Kohen, 2012; McCarty, 2003; Morcom, 2013, 2014; Preston, 2016). ILI programs are found worldwide, with the longest-running and most well-known examples established in New Zealand and Hawai'i (Ball, 2007; DeJong, 1998; Greymorning, 1995; Guèvremont & Kohen, 2012; Harrison & Papa, 2005; McCarty, 2003; McIvor, 2005; Singh & Reyhner, 2013; Wilson & Kamanā, 2011).

Indigenous Language Immersion and Academic Outcomes

Studies of these specific programs, as well as generalized studies of the academic impacts of ILI, indicate that ILI has positive impacts on students' academic and linguistic development. These studies are important because a common concern about ILI is that it will negatively impact students' ability to learn vital content and develop sufficient academic fluency in the mainstream language (Bournot-Trites & Tellowitz, 2002; White, 2015; Wright & Taylor, 1995). The impact of immersion on academic development is not just a concern for ILI but is a consideration for immersion education globally (Bournot-Trites & Tellowitz, 2002; Genesee & Jared, 2008).

Research on literacy and numeracy as well as general academic success in ILI have shed light on the question of impact. With respect to specific literacy and numeracy development, students in ILI consistently show delayed literacy development initially but then catch up and even surpass their peers, with transfer of literacy skills from the immersion language to the mainstream language (Raham, 2010; Usborne, Caoette, Qumaaluk, & Taylor, 2009; Wright & Taylor, 1995). With respect to general academic outcomes as measured through standardized test results and high school graduation rates, studies of ILI programs show positive outcomes (McCarty, 2013; Preston, 2016; Wilson & Kamanā, 2011; White, 2015). As Wilson and Kamanā (2011) write, "programs that use the Indigenous language and its heritage to an exceptional level, including full immersion . . . produce the same (or better) results in the nationally dominant language and academics as standard English-medium programs . . . for Indigenous students" (p. 51). In Canada, Indigenous students who speak an Indigenous language tend to do better overall in school and have higher high school completion rates than nonspeakers, and this effect is magnified if students also learn the Indigenous language in school (Guèvremont & Kohen, 2012). This outcome is consistent with what we know about language acquisition and bilingual education generally, and in particular is in keeping with Cummins's Threshold Hypothesis. Cummins (1976, 1979) states that once learners achieve a threshold of bilingual competence with fluency in one language, ILI will not produce negative consequences; and once students achieve fluency in both languages, bilingualism will produce positive cognitive effects. Negative cognitive effects occur when students develop low levels of competence in both languages (Cummins, 1976, 1979; Lasagabaster, 1998; Lindholm-Leary & Howard, 2008; Wilson & Kamanā, 2011).

Still, ILI is not a panacea and is not without risks. ILI programs often serve communities that have significant social and economic challenges. Students in such communities are at risk of lower academic performance and school success (Ball, 2007; Guèvremont & Kohen, 2012; Wilson & Kamanā, 2011). Furthermore, the intergenerational trauma of residential schools impacts the success of ILI and CSP. Certainly:

> It is not surprising that, faced with terrible conditions and mostly ineffective teaching, many students left [residential] school as soon as they could. A 2010 study of Aboriginal parents and children living off-reserves found that the high school completion rate is lower for residential school students (28%) than for those who did not attend (36%) (TRC, 2015b).

Because of their experiences, some survivors may not see the value of formal education, even in an Indigenous context (Ball, 2007). They also may not be able to pass on strong academic English or Indigenous language skills to their children due to their own limited educational experience or punishment for speaking their language while at residential school (TRC, 2015b). Cummins's Threshold Hypothesis predicts that students with limited proficiency in their first language, whether in English or an Indigenous language, may not benefit from immersion (Cummins, 1976, 1979; Lasagabaster, 1998; Lindholm-Leary & Howard, 2008; Wilson & Kamanā, 2011).

In some communities, existing educational, economic, and social issues, coupled with a lack of funding for education and challenges in school administration, have resulted in poor educational outcomes for students in both mainstream and ILI programs (AFN, 2010; Guèvremont & Kohen, 2012; Kipp, 2000; Morcom, 2014). Low high school graduation rates and post-secondary attendance rates, coupled with low speaker numbers, can result in a lack of trained teachers, administrators, and curriculum developers (Wilson & Kamanā, 2011). Funding and staffing shortages often mean that students must transition at some point from immersion to mainstream language schooling, and the transition can significantly and negatively impact learners in areas of Indigenous language acquisition, academic achievement, and self-esteem (Bougie, Wright, & Taylor, 2003; Guèvremont & Kohen, 2012; Wilson & Kamanā, 2011; White, 2015). For these reasons, longitudinal studies that monitor development during and after immersion education are vital.

The MMAK Within Indigenous Early Childhood Education and Immersion Models

The MMAK, an enrichment strong bilingual education (immersion) program, is an example of CSP and ILI early childhood education. Children arrive at the program with limited or no knowledge of Anishinaabemowin, and they are exposed to the language for the whole day. The program goal is additive bilingualism, or fluency in both Anishinaabemowin and English (Hornberger, 1991; Usborne et al., 2009). Within the larger field of language education and bilingual education, strong bilingual education is frequently compared to weak bilingual education, where students arrive at school primarily speaking their Indigenous language, which is used to transition them to the mainstream language classroom (Hornberger, 1991; Usborne et al., 2009).

Other approaches in the sphere of bilingual, immersion, and language education involve the concurrent use of both languages in the classroom and language teaching, where learners are directly taught the structure, function, and vocabulary of the language (Morcom, 2014). While a detailed discussion of all models is not within the scope of this article, it is important to note that they fall along a continuum. Programs may vary in how they execute similar models; in other words, two classrooms that use immersion may incorporate very different pedagogies and curricula (Hornberger, 1991). This diversity is a benefit, since CSP and ILI at their best vary to reflect the cultural values, norms, and intellectual traditions of the communities they serve (Preston, 2016).

The MMAK Model: Development and Approach

The MMAK is part of a larger move to revitalize the Anishinaabemowin language on Manitoulin Island. At the heart of Anishinaabe traditional territory in Lake Huron, Manitoulin Island is home to numerous First Nations. Six nations—Aundek Omni Kaning, Sheguiandah, M'Chigeeng, Sheshegwaning, Whitefish River, and Zhiibaahaasing—have come together under the umbrella of the United Chiefs and Council of Mnidoo Mnising (UCCMM). While Anishinaabemowin is not currently considered an endangered language (UNESCO, 2014), in the UCCMM's member Nations, only 8% of residents speak it at home while 95% believe it is important to learn the language (Pitawanakwat, 2013). To increase the use of the language in the communities, the UCCMM developed and formalized their Anishinaabek Language Declaration in the fall of 2011. The declaration asserts the right of access to the language and the intent to offer access to all services, including education, in the language to all member Nations' citizens by 2030 (UCCMM, 2013).

Following the declaration, planning commenced to develop and run the MMAK through the UCCMM's affiliate Kenjgewin Teg Educational Institute (KTEI). KTEI has been offering educational programs since 1994. All programs are based in Anishinaabe knowledge and culture. The Institute has developed the Anishinaabe Odziiwin (living language and culture) cultural standards, which are a set of guidelines and goals to help students and staff develop as Anishinaabek people (KTEI, 2016). KTEI offers programming at the elementary and secondary levels as well as post-secondary programs in partnership with mainstream colleges and universities in English and Anishinaabemowin. The institution has a large staff of educators. Community members, elders, and parents at both KTEI and in the community have also helped MMAK develop. Community engagement is vital since, as Preston (2016) points out, the tremendous diversity of Indigenous peoples in Canada means that no "one size fits all" model will serve all language immersion programs.

Parents and community members need to take an influential role in the development, promotion, and administration of the early learning programs within their community and thus ensure that the community's culture is reflected in individualized programs and an integrated curriculum that are centered on the mental, physical, spiritual, and emotional needs of the Aboriginal child (Preston, 2016). UCCMM support of the MMAK is directly responsive to the TRC's Call to Action 62, iii: "Provide the necessary funding to Aboriginal schools to utilize Indigenous knowledge and teaching methods in classrooms" (TRC, 2015a).

The MMAK began in 2013 when 12 students entered the junior kindergarten level (JK). In 2014–2015, the program expanded to include JK, senior kindergarten (SK), and a language nest for preschoolers. The school is located in the Ojibwe Cultural Foundation building on M'Chigeeng First Nation. This location is central for all of the UCCMM's member Nations and is within walking distance of KTEI's main campus. Children who live far from the school, particularly those in other First Nations, have access to bussing to allow them to attend.

Currently, the MMAK is considered a pilot project, and financial constraints limit it to the primary years (JK to Grade 3). After Grade 3, students transition to the local First Nations English-medium schools in their communities. These schools also engage traditional pedagogies and consistently integrate Anishinaabe culture and knowledge, but rather than employing immersion, students are taught the language in Anishinaabemowin classes. To help students transition to English-medium schools, the MMAK teaches JK–Grade 1 in Anishinaabemowin, and then introduces English slowly; Grade 2 is taught 80% in Anishinaabemowin, and Grade 3 is taught 50% in Anishinaabemowin and 50% in English. This graduated model is based on previous research that indicates that a sudden transition between languages can be detrimental to students' educational and personal development (Bougie, Wright, & Taylor, 2003).

Teacher Attributes and Pedagogy

A large part of the success realized in the MMAK to date can be attributed to certified teachers in the program who possess strong teacher qualities and pedagogical skills. According to Bishop, Berryman, and Richardson (2002) and McGee and Fraser (2001), effective teachers possess core teaching or pedagogical qualities including:

> a depth of knowledge about subject area, passion for what they teach, a strong desire to share knowledge, a clear philosophy of teaching and teaching goals, a commitment to developing students' understanding and growth, use of non-confrontational behaviour management strategies, a genuine interest in students as individuals, provision of high quality feedback, comforting and challenging communication of high expectations, and continual reflection on their own teaching. (p.68)

Not surprisingly, teachers in the MMAK exhibit these attributes. The authors of this paper observed these teacher effectiveness factors in many classroom visits.

MMAK teachers conduct themselves in a professional manner to make a positive difference for students and families. In addition to their work in the classroom, they teach hands-on Anishinaabemowin language learning in family-based settings in the evenings and on weekends. They also colead monthly parent meetings. The teachers are patient and caring with students and welcoming to all parents and visitors. They possess effective pedagogical qualities; for example, they plan and prepare inquiry stations, documentation and assessments, and they use a play-based pedagogical model that was implemented throughout all Ministry of Education schools in Ontario in 2014. Teachers use effective behavior management, such as a problem-solving approach that encourages students to work collectively to resolve conflicts through understanding and empathy. The teacher's role is that of a facilitator, observer, and documenter. The teacher continually questions children in ways that incite further thought and action while students are playing. For example, as we observed, a question to a child in the building block centre can be as simple as "Aaniish waa zhichige'in?" (What are you doing?) The child responds with an answer such as "Nishke shkode daabaan maaba" (Look, this is a train) while pointing to his or her train made with wooden blocks. The child drew his or her learning and then explained the picture of the train in front of the class using primarily Anishinaabemowin with sporadic English. This learning time was documented by taking pictures of the structure. The documentation contributes to the depth of the learning gained by the child from his or her self-selected investigations and by making children aware that their efforts are important and valued. Recorded visual and audio documentation provides information about children's learning and progress that cannot be demonstrated by typical tests and checklists.

The teachers use the heritage language continuously, in context, whether in the form of a greeting in the morning, teaching math at the circle, instructing letters and sounds at the literacy centre using sticks, playing outdoors under the trees in a student-made fort, participating in physical education, or having a hot lunch and snacks together. As an example, during the daily routines and rituals, which include smudging with sage, all students gather together in circle-time so they start the day in a good way. They recite the Anishinaabemowin thanksgiving called, "Mii manda enweying" (This is who we are), a preamble developed by the United Chiefs and Councils Elder's Council; sing hand drum songs, such as the water song, that have been handed down through the generations; and share who they are, where they come from, and how they are feeling. Students can introduce themselves in the language such as: "Carter ndishnikaz; niiwin ndaa zaaboongis, M'Chigeeng ndoon jibaa. Sherry miinwaa John ngitziimak, ngi chi nendam nongwa" (My name is Carter. I am four years old. I am from M'Chigeeng. My parents are Sherry and John, and I am happy today.) They may bring in items to share, show their drawings, or speak freely with the teachers, who ask guiding questions of the children in their language. These types of questions or comments to the children help them over time understand the heritage language in context, and they in turn start to use the new vocabulary in the language. Having two teachers and additional speakers from the communities in the school is critical so that students hear the language in a rich way by processing and engaging in dialogue frequently and in context. An example we observed was a teacher saying "gojiing kaa zhaami" (Let's go outside). The students were then able to use this vocabulary and sentence structure, showing communication skills in their heritage language.

The teachers' approach aligns with Anishinaabe teaching practice, which is as much as possible child-initiated and child-led. The time schedule is less structured than many schools (no bells) and risk taking is encouraged. In this environment, children have an element of control over their learning environment, experience real life problem solving, and develop responsibility, pride, and a sense of cooperation. Traditional Anishinaabe education involves learning through trial and error and acute observation of the environment; these methods invoke natural curiosity and learning within the safety and careful watch of loving caregivers, extended family, and community. The teachers are very proficient in immersion methods and use an oral language-focused approach for comprehension, understanding, and vocabulary development with the children.

The MMAK teachers are passionate about their work. Despite a heavy workload, training challenges, and time constraints, the teachers focus on supporting the children and ensuring the survival of the Anishinaabe language and culture. They share a clear teaching philosophy and teaching goals. *Experiential learning*, hands-on methods in all curricular subjects, engages students in doing rather than in studying. *Inquiry-based learning* ensures children have a sense of discovery, wonder, and awe in the learning process. Teachers also focus on holistic and *integrated learning*—a single lesson using an interdisciplinary approach that can meet objectives in more than one subject area. For example, a visit to the river or picking medicines during the spring and fall in the local woods meets curriculum expectations in physical education, social studies, and science. A theme of environmental stewardship across subject areas means that students learn *about* the environment, *for* the environment, and *in* the environment. For example, students study and pick plants, such as *zhngobiins* (juniper), which is used during flu season, or they plant a garden of beans, tomatoes, and strawberries. These themes are in keeping with the sacred laws of the Anishinaabe, who are caretakers for Mother Earth. In aesthetic terms, the indoor classroom and the playground feature natural and recycled materials with a focus on local environment and Indigenous art. Students spend a great deal of time learning on the land; fieldtrips engage them in seasonal outdoor cultural practices such as fishing, medicine picking, playing Indigenous games (lacrosse, doubleball), and producing maple syrup.

The MMAK pedagogy is inspired by the Reggio Emilia approach (Malaguzzi, 1998), which has been adapted to suit Anishinaabe pedagogy. Rather than preparing lesson plans beforehand, teachers guide learning based on the children's interests by creating spaces for educational exploration. They integrate graphic arts and focus on cognitive, social, and language development. The goal is for the children to become active participants in learning, engaging all their senses and developing the ability to discover, question, and grow as learners. The role of the teachers in this distinctive learning environment is to move from instructor to facilitator, providing a safe and nurturing setting so that children can discover, interact, and interpret the world around them with a sense of curiosity and wonder.

Family and Community Attributes and Pedagogy

Research on other Early Childhood Education (ECE) immersion programs indicates that a family-based approach with Elder support enhances success for ILI and CSP programs (Aylward, 2009; Chodkiewicz, Widin, & Yasukawa, 2008; Guillory & Williams, 2014; Preston, 2016). MMAK families contribute to an effective home-school partnership. Parents and caregivers participate in field trips and classroom events, and teachers create relationships with whole families, encourage cooperative problem solving, and promote respect for everyone who enters the classroom. Their partnership reflects respect for land, language, culture, and traditional spirituality, affirming the importance of an Anishinaabe worldview that values interrelations. Elders and knowledge keepers visit the classroom regularly, teaching about ceremonies, drumming, winter stories, traditional medicine, and other traditional knowledge. Visitors teach Anishinaabe content using Anishinaabe pedagogies, and since many are fluent (even first-language) Anishinaabemowin speakers, students can experience fluent speech in conversation.

Research with the MMAK

Since the MMAK is a pilot project, parents, teachers, and administrators requested that we engage in research to inform program development and to share insights with other communities who are exploring ILI. Our research goals are threefold: (a) to assess students' acquisition of Anishinaabemowin as a second language, (b) to assess students' cultural pride and personal self-esteem as young learners, and (c) to assess students' academic development to ensure the program meets their learning needs. In this article, we focus on the children's academic development. Assessment of participants' Anishinaabemowin language development is detailed in Morcom and Roy (2017), and details of students' self-esteem development are discussed in Morcom (forthcoming). The research will continue until at least 2018–2019, when the current cohort of students will complete Grade 3, after which they will transition to an English-medium school.

Positionality

We are connected to this research through academic interest and personal relations. Anishinaabek kwe Stephanie Roy of the Crane clan has been a researcher, doctoral student, executive director, parent, and governing council member of KTEI. She is a lifelong resident of M'Chigeeng First Nation in the heart of Manitoulin Island, where the total population of approximately 10,000 people is about 50% Native and 50% non-Native. Lindsay A. Morcom is Anishinaabe Métis and a member of the Bear clan. She is a professor of education and coordinator of the Aboriginal Teacher Education Program (ATEP) at Queen's University. KTEI and ATEP have a long-standing relationship, as KTEI provides space and support for the Manitoulin-North Shore community-based ATEP program. In addition to coauthoring articles on the MMAK, we work closely together on the management and delivery of ATEP. We are proud of our Anishinaabe heritage; we share a personal commitment to work for the preservation and propagation of our language and to identify best practices for the education of our children and all other Indigenous children. This research is part of a multifaceted longitudinal study funded by an Insight Grant from the Social Sciences and Humanities Research Council of Canada (SSHRC).

Ethical Considerations

In keeping with the principles of ownership, control, access, and possession (OCAP) (First Nations Information Governance Centre, 2016), this research was developed in collaboration with the MMAK teachers and community members. The research plan was approved by the Queen's University General Research Ethics Board. Prior to publication in any form, the results have been presented to the families, teachers of the MMAK students, and the wider community. Findings have also been presented to the chief and council of M'Chigeeng First Nation, where the MMAK is located. Because our study participant pool is so small, we do not include specific identifying or performance information about any participant in any publication. In our analysis and results, we only discuss trends within the participant pool.

Methodology

Participants. The participant pool for the study included 12 JK students—seven boys and five girls—all of whom are First Nations and living on-reserve. All started school with the MMAK in September 2013; we refer to this cohort as Cohort A. None spoke Anishinaabemowin as a first language, and none had attended language nests or been formally educated in Anishinaabemowin prior to joining the MMAK. The children were tested in Spring 2014, when all were four or five years old. In the 2014–2015 academic year, three of Cohort A left the school, and one research participant, a non-Indigenous boy, joined the school in February 2015 at the SK level. At the conclusion of the 2014–2015 academic year, Cohort A included 10 students—seven boys and three girls.

Five study participants joined the MMAK in the 2014–2015 academic year at the JK level; we refer to this group as Cohort B. Cohort B included four students—three girls and one boy—all First Nations and living on-reserve. Cohort B also includes one non-Indigenous boy who joined the MMAK in February 2015 at the JK level. Like Cohort A, none of these students spoke Anishinaabemowin as a first language, and none had been formally educated in the language prior to joining the MMAK. All participants were in good overall health with no known physical or learning challenges.

Purpose and research question. The research sought to identify whether ILI in the MMAK negatively or positively impacts students' academic development, as measured using the EYE-TA.

Procedure. Academic development was evaluated using the EYE-TA, which was administered once per year in the spring by a research assistant. The research assistant, who was trained to administer the EYE-TA, is a qualified teacher who works as an educator with KTEI but who is not one of the regular MMAK teachers. The tests were individually administered to each child. The EYE-TA requires the child to perform specific tasks; performance is rated on a scale of one to four, according to specific set criteria. The study used EYE-TA because (a) it is used at other UCCMM schools and other schools in the region;

(b) rather than focusing only on cognitive development, it evaluates children on a holistic basis that is consistent with Anishinaabe values; (c) it compares children to a larger pool of similarly-aged children, rather than comparing them with classmates of different ages; (d) it is appropriate for holistic evaluation in a play-based learning environment; and (e) the class and individual child reports that are produced are clear, practical, and useful to parents, teachers, and researchers.

The EYE-TA evaluates students in the following areas (Early Years Evaluation, 2016):

- Awareness of self and environment: a child's understanding of his or her environment and the ability to make connections between experiences in school, home, and the community
- Social skills and learning approaches: a child's ability to pay attention during learning activities, interact with peers, and behave according to classroom expectations
- Cognitive skills: basic numeracy, pre-literacy, and problem solving skills
- Language and communication: a child's understanding of spoken language and use of expressive language
- Fine motor development: a child's hand-eye coordination and ability to perform tasks requiring small movements
- Gross motor development: a child's ability to use his or her arms, legs, and body to perform tasks requiring larger movements

Analysis. The EYE-TA scores were analyzed quantitatively. EYE-TA assessment data, along with each child's date of birth (to determine age in months and years) were entered into an online analysis program, which generated a report specific to each child as well as a general report on the progress of the class. Scores were reported numerically for each child in each area. A score above 2.00 is ranked at Tier 3, indicating age-appropriate development in a given area; a score from 1.00–1.99 is ranked at Tier 2, indicating that a child is experiencing some difficulty in that area and requires more targeted interventions; and a score from 0.00–0.99 is ranked at Tier 1, indicating significant difficulty and a need for intensive additional intervention (EYE, 2016).

By calculating the average scores for each cohort in each area, we determined whether the cohort was on average performing at or below age-appropriate expectations in each area. We also examined median scores and standard deviations to identify whether the averages were influenced significantly by outliers or whether all members of the cohort showed similar development.

Results

Across both cohorts, the average of the individual student scores at the JK level is on par with age-appropriate expectations in every area except the cognitive skills tested by the EYE-TA. Within the EYE-TA, cognitive skill includes basic math, preliteracy, and problem-solving skills. For example, children are asked to name letters and sounds, count numbers, and identify patterns. Note that we use the term *cognitive skill* to be consistent with the terminology used in the EYE-TA metric; when we say scores were below age-appropriate development in cognitive skill, this refers only to the EYE-TA metric and does not indicate that these children show any pathological cognitive deficit. In Cohort B, student average scores were also slightly below age-appropriate expectations in language and communication, which refers to a child's ability to understand and express him- or herself in spoken language (EYE, 2016). Table 1 shows Cohort A's average and median scores at the JK level as well as the standard deviation in the scores. Table 2 contains the same results for Cohort B in JK.

Table 1. Results for Cohort A at the Junior Kindergarten Level

	Awareness of self and environment	Social skills and learning approaches	Cognitive skill	Language and communication	Fine motor	Gross motor
Average	2.40	2.39	1.53	2.57	2.17	2.63
Median	2.50	2.38	1.38	2.66	2.40	2.63
Standard deviation	.40	.30	.86	.41	.52	.42

Table 2. Results for Cohort B at the Junior Kindergarten Level

	Awareness of self and environment	Social skills and learning approaches	Cognitive skill	Language and communication	Fine motor	Gross motor
Average	2.05	2.15	1.28	1.88	2.28	2.60
Median	2.00	2.25	1.38	1.88	2.20	2.80
Standard deviation	.13	.52	.99	.45	.09	.38

Table 3. Results for All Junior Kindergarten Students

	Awareness of self and environment	Social skills and learning approaches	Cognitive skill	Language and communication	Fine motor	Gross motor
Average	2.28	2.31	1.41	2.34	2.19	2.62
Median	2.50	2.38	1.38	2.50	2.40	2.80
Standard deviation	0.37	0.36	0.87	0.51	0.43	0.39

Table 4. Results for Cohort A at the Senior Kindergarten Level

	Awareness of self and environment	Social skills and learning approaches	Cognitive skill	Language and communication	Fine motor	Gross motor
Average	2.55	2.19	2.36	2.49	2.42	2.66
Median	2.57	2.07	2.69	2.63	2.50	2.80
Standard deviation	0.20	0.33	0.73	0.48	0.47	0.37

For both cohorts, the standard deviation in the category of cognitive skill is high, indicating a wide range of scores. While some students in each cohort scored high in cognitive skill, other students were experiencing some or significant difficulty. The standard deviation is lower across Cohort B in the area of language and cognition; two students scored at Tier 3, two scored at Tier 2, and none scored at Tier 1. Taking Cohorts A and B together, Table 3 indicates average and median scores for MMAK students at the JK level.[1]

In SK, Cohort A showed age-appropriate development in every area on the EYE-TA with respect to their average and median scores, as Table 4 shows.

The standard deviation remains high in the area of cognitive skill, as one student scored at Tier 1 and another scored at Tier 2. However, the majority of students (83%) demonstrated age-appropriate development in all areas. Table 5 compares average scores in all areas between JK (Cohorts A and B taken together) and SK (Cohort A):

Table 5. Results by Year

	Awareness of self and environment	Social skills and learning approaches	Cognitive skill	Language and communication	Fine motor	Gross motor
JK Average	2.40	2.33	1.70	2.52	2.04	2.50
SK Average	2.55	2.36	2.50	2.42	2.66	2.19

Discussion

Academic results for the first two years of this program are encouraging. The radar chart in Figure 1 illustrates the development of Cohort A students in JK and SK, and Cohort B students in JK.

As Figure 1 shows, on average JK students in Cohort B were at Tier 2, or below age-appropriate expectations, in the EYE-TA area of language and communication. In JK, both cohorts were at Tier 2 in the EYE-TA area of cognitive skill. SK students were at Tier 3 in all areas, which indicates age-appropriate development.

Findings for language and communication: The ability to understand spoken English and express oneself in English. To test receptive language skills, students were evaluated for how well they understood instructions, engaged in conversation, and understood stories. To test expressive language skills, students were evaluated to see whether they were able to form full sentences that others could understand, and whether they could express how they were feeling. Receptive and expressive language skills in English are important because these children will be transitioning to English-medium school in Grade 4 and will need communicative fluency in English to thrive there. Importantly, positive outcomes can address local and wider concerns that immersion education in Anishinaabemowin or any other heritage language might hinder English language acquisition (Bournot-Trites & Tellowitz, 2002; Wright & Taylor, 1995).

Our data show that SK Cohort A students learning in Anishinaabemowin exhibit age-appropriate development in English language and communication skills. In JK, Cohort B were slightly below age-appropriate expectations in English language and communication, with an average score of 1.88. Cohort B scores fall in line with existing research, which indicates that children may experience a short period of adjustment in their language use when beginning ILI, but they

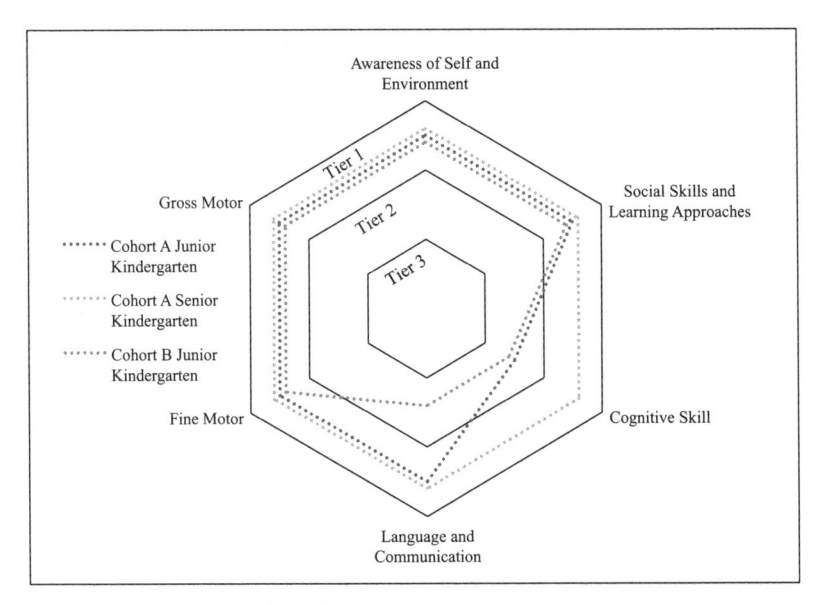

Figure 1. Comparison of results.

quickly catch up to an age-appropriate level (McCarty, 2013; Preston, 2016; Raham, 2010; Usborne et al., 2009; White, 2015; Wilson & Kamanā, 2011; Wright & Taylor, 1995). Our results indicate that attending school in an ILI setting is not detrimental to a child's language development in English. As Wright and Taylor (1995) state, "The common assumption that the use of the heritage language will negatively affect the acquisition of English skills is clearly false. In fact, there is evidence that heritage language instruction may result in better performance in English in the long run" (p. 241). In our study, in keeping with Cummins's Threshold Hypothesis, the students demonstrate additive bilingualism—knowledge transfer from one language to the other—such that their overall linguistic development remains on par with age expectations (Cummins, 1976, 1979; Lasagabaster, 1998; Lindholm-Leary & Howard, 2008; Wilson & Kamanā, 2011).

Findings for cognitive skills. Average scores for both cohorts were below age-appropriate expectations with respect to cognitive skill on the EYE-TA in JK. However, this rose to an average of 2.49 for Cohort A in SK and is one of their stronger areas of development. The rise in scores from JK to SK is also in keeping with findings of previous research: children in ILI often experience slowed development in literacy and numeracy in the beginning but normally catch up and often surpass their peers who have not been in ILI (Raham, 2010; Wright & Taylor, 1995; Usborne et al., 2009). As they develop fluency, children in ILI are able to transfer skills and knowledge acquired in one language to the other language.

Limitations

This study is subject to limitations. First, the sample size is small due to space and financial constraints on the program. Also, results may not be generalizable because the MMAK uses the distinctive and novel approach of an Anishinaabe-informed Reggio Emilia pedagogy with two gifted teachers. No two classrooms will ever be identical in their approaches or their outcomes. The results reported here cannot be immediately generalized across populations, but they meaningfully expand our limited knowledge of ILI models and can thus inform educational and financial policy for First Nations education (Chambers, 2014). The research reported here continues in a longitudinal study that will follow these students over at least four years to determine long-term impacts and contribute to the scholarship about language instruction and immersion methods.

Conclusion

What impact does Anishinaabemowin ILI in the MMAK have on students' academic development, as measured holistically using the EYE-TA? MMAK students' average scores demonstrate age-appropriate development by the end of their second year in ILI, and in fact, cognitive skill becomes one of the participants' strongest areas of development. This finding is significant because Indigenous children often exhibit disconcerting lower levels of school achievement compared to non-Indigenous children in Canada. Far from hindering students' academic development, ILI schooling may help them to flourish.

Our data contravene the common concern that ILI may have a negative impact on students' ability to respond to academic tasks presented in English and may hamper their English language acquisition (Bournot-Trites & Tellowitz, 2002; Wright & Taylor, 1995). The participants in this study demonstrate age-appropriate English language development by the end of their second year. Students in the MMAK demonstrate additive bilingualism, or robust language acquisition in both their first language (in this case, English) and the target language

(Anishinaabemowin) in keeping with Cummins's Threshold Hypothesis (Cummins, 1976, 1979; Lasagabaster, 1998; Lindholm-Leary & Howard, 2008; Wilson & Kamanā, 2011). Our findings reinforce the results of ILI research globally; consistently, we find that students may experience some academic or language delay upon starting school in an ILI environment but that with time, these students catch up and may even surpass expectations (McCarty, 2013; Preston, 2016; Raham, 2010; Usborne et al., 2009; White, 2015; Wilson & Kamanā, 2011; Wright & Taylor, 1995). As White (2015) explains:

> The belief that language immersion will hinder academic success must be dispelled. The future of indigenous language survival is at stake. Some language immersion students may fall behind temporarily . . . but the majority catches up quickly and excels beyond expectations in their academic and social lives. (p. 174)

Our results suggest that ILI may help overcome challenges in educational achievement that are of concern in Indigenous communities and that impact all of Canadian society. Still, First Nations may face significant barriers in developing ILI education given the chronic underfunding of First Nations schools in Canada (Morcom, 2014). However, in this era of reconciliation, Canadians owe it to First Nations children to move beyond resource constraints and to develop educational policy based on a renewed commitment to honour our treaties and respect our nation-to-nation relationships. Our shared goal must be to ensure that First Nations children have all the support they need to grow into confident learners who are armed with deep cultural and linguistic knowledge and who have the skills and resources to succeed in any path they choose.

Lindsay A. Morcom *(Bear Clan) is assistant professor and Aboriginal Teacher Education Program Coordinator at Queen's University. She holds a doctorate in linguistics from Oxford University, and is a Rhodes Scholar. Her research areas include Aboriginal education, education for reconciliation, linguistics, and language revitalization.*

Stephanie Roy *(Crane Clan) is executive director of Kenjgewin Teg Educational Institute. She holds degrees from Laurentian University, Queen's University, and the University of Toronto, and is currently working toward her doctorate at the Ontario Institute for Studies in Education. She has twenty years of experience in Indigenous education.*

NOTES

Our thanks to the children, families, and teachers of the MMAK for their support of this research. *Chi-miigwech*. Research was funded by an Insight Grant from the Social Sciences and Humanities Research Council of Canada.

1. The average (or mean) is the sum of the scores divided by the number of scores. The median is the middle value in the list of scores. Standard deviation measures the variation in the scores; the higher the standard deviation, the more variation there is in the list of scores.

REFERENCES

Agbo, S. (2001). Enhancing success in American Indian students: Participatory research at Akwesasne as part of a culturally relevant curriculum. *Journal of American Indian Education, 40* (1), 31–56.

Assembly of First Nations. (2010). *First Nations control of First Nations education*. Retrieved from http://www.afn.ca/uploads/files/education/3._2010_july_afn_first_nations_control_of_first_nations_education_final_eng.pdf

Aylward, M. L. (2009). Journey to Inuuqatigiit: Curriculum development for Nunavut education. *Diaspora, Indigenous, and Minority Education, 3*(3), 137–158.

Ball, J. (2007). *Aboriginal young children's language and literacy development: Research evaluating progress, promising practices, and needs*. Canadian Language and Literacy Networked Centre of Excellence. Retrieved from http://www.ecdip.org/docs/pdf/CLLRNet %20Feb%202008.pdf

Battiste, M. (2013). *Decolonizing education: Nourishing the learning spirit*. Saskatoon, SK, Canada: Purich Publishing.

Bishop, R., Berryman, M., & Richardson, C. (2002). Te toi huarewa: Effective teaching and learning in total immersion Maori language educational settings. *Canadian Journal of Native Education, 26*(1), 44–61.

Bougie, É., Wright, S., & Taylor, D. (2003). Early heritage-language education and the abrupt shift to a dominant-language classroom: Impact on the personal and collective esteem of Inuit children in Arctic Québec. *International Journal of Bilingual Education and Bilingualism, 6* (5), 349–373.

Bournot-Trites, M. & Tellowitz, U. (2002). *Report of current research on the effects of second language learning on first language literacy skills*. Halifax, NS, Canada: The Atlantic Provinces Educational Foundation. Retrieved from https://www.acpi.ca/documents/report.pdf/

Campbell, L. (1997). *American Indian languages: The historical linguistics of Native America*. Oxford, UK: Oxford University Press.

Canada. Statistics Canada. (2011). Fact sheet—2011 National household survey Aboriginal demographics, educational attainment and labour market outcomes. 27 December 2016. Retrieved from https://www.aadnc-aandc.gc.ca/eng/1376329205785 /1376329233875

Chambers, N. A. (2014). *"They all talk Okanagan and I know what they are saying": Language nests in the early years: Insights, challenges, and promising practices*. (Unpublished doctoral dissertation). Kelowna, BC, Canada: University of British Columbia Okanagan.

Chodkiewicz, A., Widin, J., & Yasukawa, K. (2008). Engaging Aboriginal families to support student and community learning. *Diaspora, Indigenous, and Minority Education, 2*(1), 64–81.

Cummins, J. (1976). The influence of bilingualism on cognitive growth: A synthesis of research findings and explanatory hypotheses. *Working Papers on Bilingualism, 9*. Retrieved from http://files.eric.ed.gov/fulltext/ED125311.pdf

Cummins, J. (1979). Linguistic interdependence and the educational development of bilingual children. *Review of Educational Research, 49*, 221–251.

DeJong, D. H. (1998). Is immersion the key to language renewal? *Journal of American Indian Education, 37*(3), 31–46.

Demmert, W. G. (2001). *Improving academic performance among Native American students: A review of the research literature.* Charleston, SC: ERIC Clearinghouse on Rural Education and Small Schools.

Early Years Evaluation. (2016). Early years evaluation—Teacher assessment (EYE-TA). 12 December 2016. Retrieved from https://www.earlyyearsevaluation.com/index.php /en/products/eye-ta

First Nations Information Governance Centre. (2016, Dec. 10). The First Nations principles of ownership, control, access, and possession. Retrieved from http://fnigc.ca/ocap.html

Genesee, F. & Jared, D. (2008). Literacy development in early French immersion programs. *Canadian Psychology, 49*(2), 140–147. doi: 10.1037/0708-5591.49.2.140

Grenoble, L., & Whaley, L. J. (2006). *Saving languages: An introduction to language revitalization.* Cambridge, UK: Cambridge University Press.

Greymorning, S. (1995). Going beyond words: The Arapaho immersion program. In J. Reyhner (Ed.), *Teaching Indigenous languages.* (pp. 22–30). Flagstaff, AZ: Northern Arizona University.

Guèvremont, A., & Kohen, D. E. (2012). Knowledge of an Aboriginal language and school outcomes for children and adults. *International Journal of Bilingual Education and Bilingualism, 15*(1), 1–27.

Guillory, R. M., & Williams, G. L. (2014). Incorporating the culture of American Indian/Alaska Native students into the classroom. *Diaspora, Indigenous, and Minority Education, 8*(3), 155–169.

Harrison, B., & Papa, R. (2005). The development of an Indigenous knowledge program in a New Zealand Maori-language immersion school. *Anthropology and Education Quarterly, 36*(1), 57–72.

Hermes, M., Bang, M., & Marin, A. (2012). Designing Indigenous language revitalization. *Harvard Educational Review, 82*(3), 381–402.

Hornberger, N. H. (1991). Extending enrichment bilingual education: Revisiting typologies and redirecting policy. In O. García (Ed.), *Bilingual education: Fosschrift in honor of Joshua A. Fishman.* vol. 1, (pp. 215–234). Amsterdam: John Benjamins.

Kenjgewin Teg Educational Institute. (2016). *KTEI Anishinaabe Odziiwin FAQs.* Retrieved from http://www.ktei.net/faqs---anishinabe-odziiwin-passport.html

Kipp. D. (2000). *Encouragement, guidance, insights, and lessons learned for Native language activists developing their own tribal language programs.* Browning, MT: Peigan Institute. Retrieved from http://www.rnld.org/sites/default/files/Kipp%202000.pdf

Lasagabaster, D. (1998). The threshold hypothesis applied to three languages in contact at school. *Bilingual Education and Bilingualism, 1*(2), 119–133.

Lindholm-Leary, K., & Howard, E. (2008). Language development and academic achievement in two-way immersion programs. In T. Williams Fortune & D. J. Tedick, (Eds.), *Pathways to multilingualism: Evolving perspectives on immersion education* (pp. 177–200). Clevedon, UK: Multilingual Matters.

Lockard, L. & de Groat, J. (2010). "He said it all in Navajo!": Indigenous language immersion in early childhood classrooms. *International Journal of Multicultural Education, 12*(2), 1–14.

Louis, W., & Taylor, D. M. (2001). When the survival of a language is at stake: The future of Inuttitut in Arctic Quebec. *Journal of Language and Psychology, 20*(1&2), 111–143.

Malaguzzi, L. (1998). History, ideas and basic philosophy. In C. Edwards, L. Gandini, and G. Forman (Eds.), *The hundred languages of children: The Reggio Emilia approach—Advanced reflections,* 2nd ed, (pp. 49–98). Greenwich, UK: Ablex Publishing.

McCarty, T. L. (2003). Revitalizing Indigenous languages in homogenising times. *Comparative Education, 39*(2), Special Number 27: Indigenous education, new possibilities, ongoing constraints, 147–163.

McCarty, T. L. (2013). *Language planning and policy in Native America: History, theory, praxis.* Bristol, UK: Multilingual Matters.

McGee, C., & Fraser, D. (Eds). (2001). *The professional practice of teaching.* Palmerston North: Dunmore Press.

McIvor, O. (2005). The contribution of Indigenous heritage language immersion programs to healthy early childhood development. In C. St. Aubin (Ed.), *Compendium on Aboriginal early child development,* (pp. 5–20). Ottawa, ON, Canada: Canadian Child Care Federation.

Morcom, L. A. (2013). *Aboriginal language and school success: What can I expect for my child?* M'Chigeeng First Nation: Kenjgewin Teg Educational Institute. Retrieved from http://www.ktei.net/uploads/1/4/7/8/1478467/language_immersion_and_school_success_for_parents_-_dr._morcom.pdf

Morcom, L. A. (2014). Determining the role of language and culture in First Nations schools: A comparison of the *First Nations Education Act* with the policy of the Assembly of First Nations. *Canadian Journal of Educational Administration and Policy,* 163. Retrieved from http://www.umanitoba.ca/publications/cjeap/ pdf_files/morcom.pdf

Morcom, L. A. (forthcoming). Self-esteem and cultural identity in Aboriginal language immersion kindergarteners. *International Journal of Language, Identity, and Education.*

Morcom, L. A. & Roy, S. (2017). Is early immersion effective for Aboriginal language acquisition? A case study from an Anishinaabemowin kindergarten. *International Journal of Bilingual Education and Bilingualism.* DOI: 10.1080/13670050.2017.1281217.

Paris, D., & Alim, H. S. (2014). What are we seeking to sustain through culturally sustaining pedagogy? A loving critique forward. *Harvard Educational Review, 84*(1), 85–100.

Perley, B. C. (2011). *Defying Maliseet language death: Emergent vitalities of language, culture, and identity in Eastern Canada.* Lincoln, NE: University of Nebraska Press.

Pitawanakwat, B. (2013). *Anishinaabemowin immersion for children ages 0–10: A feasibility study and community survey report for Kenjgewin Teg Educational Institute.* (Unpublished report). Kenjgewin Teg Educational Institute: M'Chigeeng First Nation.

Preston, J. (2016). Education for Aboriginal peoples in Canada: An overview of four realms of success. *Diaspora, Indigenous, and Minority Education, 10*(1), 14–27. doi: 10.1080/15595692.2015.1084917/

Raham, H. (2010). Policy levers for improving outcomes for off-reserve students. Paper presented to the Colloquium on Improving the Educational Outcomes of Aboriginal People Living Off-Reserve. Retrieved from http://www.usask.ca/education/aboriginal/colloquium/Ses-A-Helen-Raham-paper.pdf

Singh, N. K., & Reyhner, J. (2013). Indigenous knowledge and pedagogy for Indigenous children. In J. Reyhner, L. Lockard, and W. S. Gilbert (Eds.), *Honoring our children: Culturally appropriate approaches for teaching Indigenous students* (pp. 37–52). Flagstaff, AZ: Northern Arizona University.

Truth and Reconciliation Commission of Canada. (2015a). *Calls to action.* Retrieved from http://www.trc.ca/websites/trcinstitution/File/2015/Findings/Calls_to_Action_English2.pdf

Truth and Reconciliation Commission. (2015b). *Honouring the truth, reconciling the future: Summary of the final report of the Truth and Reconciliation Commission of Canada.* Retrieved from http://www.trc.ca/websites/trcinstitution/File/2015/ Findings/Exec_Summary_2015_05_31_web_0.pdf

United Chiefs and Council of Mnidoo Mnising [UCCMM]. (2013). *Anishinaabek language declaration.* Retrieved from http://www.uccmm.ca/anishinabek-language-declaration.html

United Nations Educational, Scientific, and Cultural Organization [UNESCO]. (2014). *UNESCO Atlas of the world's languages in danger.* Retrieved from: http://www.unesco.org /culture/languages-atlas/index.php. Accessed Dec. 18, 2014.

Usborne, E., Caoette, J., Qumaaluk, Q., & Taylor, D. M. (2009). Bilingual education in an Aboriginal context: Examining the transfer of language skills from Inuttitut to English or French. *International Journal of Bilingual Education and Bilingualism, 12*(6), 667–684.

Usborne, E., Peck, J., Smith, D., & Taylor, D. M. (2011). Learning through an Aboriginal language: The impact on students' English and Aboriginal language skills. *Canadian Journal of Education, 34*(4): 200–215.

Watahomigie, L., & McCarty, T. L. (1994). Education at Peach Springs: A Hualapai way of schooling. *Peabody Journal of Education, 69*(2), 26–42.

White, L. (2015). *Free to be Mohawk: Indigenous education at the Akwesasne Freedom School*. Norman, OK: University of Oklahoma Press.

Wilson, W. H., & Kamanā, K. (2011). Insights from Indigenous language immersion in Hawai'i. In D. J. Tedick, D. Christian, & T. Williams Fortune (Eds.), *Immersion education: Practices, policies, and possibilities* (pp. 36–57). Salisbury, UK: Multilingual Matters.

Wright, S. C., & Taylor, D. M. (1995). Identity and the language of the classroom: Investigating the impact of heritage versus second language instruction on personal and collective self-esteem. *Journal of Educational Psychology, 87*(2), 241–252.

Contributor Information

The *Journal of American Indian Education* (*JAIE*) is a refereed journal publishing original scholarship about education issues of American Indians, Alaska Natives, Native Hawaiians, and Indigenous peoples worldwide, including First Nations, Māori, Aboriginal/Torres Strait Islander peoples, Indigenous peoples of Latin America, Africa, and others. *JAIE* strives to improve Indigenous education through empirical research; knowledge generation; and transmission to researchers, communities, and diverse educational settings.

JAIE encourages dialogues among researchers and practitioners through research-based articles elucidating current educational issues and innovations. *JAIE* also invites original scholarly essays advancing a point of view about an educational question or issue, when supported by cited research literature; original reviews of literature in underexplored areas; original expository manuscripts that develop or interpret a theory or issue; and Reports From the Field. Studies grounded in Indigenous research methodologies are especially encouraged.

Prepare manuscripts according to the most recent *Publication Manual of the American Psychological Association* (6th ed.) (http://www.apastyle.org/manual/index.aspx). Format manuscripts in Microsoft Word and blind for anonymous peer review; manuscripts not blinded or appropriately formatted will be returned. Authors must certify that the manuscript is not being considered by another publisher. All empirical studies must document (1) the use of accepted ethical protocols for research with human subjects, and (2) site-specific approvals, including research and/or institutional review board approvals required by Native nations, tribes, or bands as well as schools and school districts, where appropriate. Please use the term most appropriate to the Indigenous group or people to whom the manuscript refers. *American Indian/Alaska Native*, *Native American*, *Native Hawaiian*, and *Indigenous* are acceptable terms when referring to Indigenous peoples of the United States.

All manuscripts must be submitted electronically to jaie@asu.edu. Submit: (1) double-spaced manuscript as one Word document (do not send a pdf), including the title and abstract (maximum 150 words); (2) biographical statement(s) for each author (50 words each) and contact information for each author, including author name, affiliation, email address, physical street address, and phone number. Do not include author name(s) on or in the manuscript.

Feature-length Manuscripts Original scholarly manuscripts should be double-spaced, 7,500–8,000 words total, including endnotes, if any, and references.

Reports From the Field Original scholarly manuscripts providing descriptive, evaluative, and/or policy-oriented analyses of innovative education models and practices may be considered as "Reports From the Field." Reports should be up to 5,000 words, including endnotes, if any, and references. See the website and *JAIE* 49(3) for a fuller description of Reports From the Field.

Indigenous Policy Forum (IPF) Invited manuscripts. The *IPF* functions as a current conversational space and an important historical archive, featuring the voices and vision of Indigenous education policymakers, policy implementers, and activists.

Manuscripts will be considered throughout the year and, if accepted, will be published in any of the three issues at the direction of the editorial staff. There is no remuneration for *JAIE* contributors; authors will receive two free copies of the issue in which the manuscript is published. For more information, see the *JAIE* website at http://jaie.asu.edu.

JOURNAL OF AMERICAN INDIAN EDUCATION

CALL FOR PEER REVIEWERS

AS A PEER-REVIEWED JOURNAL, *JAIE* depends upon the generosity of our colleagues in the field of Indigenous education. Rigorous, constructive, and supportive peer review is essential to the health of our field and to the quality of our journal.

We invite interested academic colleagues, practitioners, and advanced doctoral students to sign up as peer reviewers for *JAIE*. Your name will be added to the database we consult for reviews of submitted manuscripts. *JAIE* uses double-blinded peer review: the identities of manuscript authors are not shared with reviewers, and the identities of peer reviewers are not shared with authors. If you are already a reviewer for the journal, please log on to the new website and fill out a Reviewer Application so we have updated information in our database.

The responsibilities of peer review include:

- Timely response to requests to review, letting the editorial assistant know if you can review the submitted manuscript

- Completion of review within three to four weeks of receiving the manuscript

- Detailed commentary on the strengths and weaknesses of the manuscript, including its contribution to knowledge, adherence to ethical standards of research, narrative and organizational coherence, and relevance of analytic or descriptive content

- Constructive and supportive suggestions to improve or enhance the manuscript.

To sign up, please visit the *JAIE* website at https://jaie.asu.edu/. At the foot of the home page, click on Reviewer Application. Fill out the fields of the online form, attach a PDF copy of your c.v., and click Submit.

Thank you!